P9-DUJ-413

Edited and designed by the editorial staff of ORTHO BOOKS

Basic research and text:
Mariel Dewey

Coordinating Editor: A. Cort Sinnes

Photography: Clyde Childress

Special Consultants: Janeth Nix and Lawrence Siegel

Front cover photograph: Fred Lyon

12 Months Harvest

Contents

From harvest to harvest

Whether you have a vegetable garden or not, here's the first hand "how-to" for a year 'round harvest.

With the increased interest in vegetable gardening, and food in general, we felt a book on food preservation would be particularly helpful to many people. Unfortunately, many of the methods of "putting food by" are becoming a lost art. As one of our consultants in Jonesville, Louisiana put it, "This is the way my Aunt Eunice taught me; these are things we all should know, but not everyone has an Aunt Eunice to tell them." With this book we hope we have, in our own way, succeeded in bringing you the kind of first hand information which few people have access to.

A book on food preservation is necessarily tied to the past. The methods of preservation described in this book (save for freezing) were at one time the only methods available for preserving food from harvest to harvest; it was essential to know these methods if a family was to eat during the winter months.

The reasons for using these methods today are varied—for some it is the desire to recall that "old-time" flavor of homemade jam, others enjoy the security of knowing exactly what has gone into the foods they eat, and still others feel a sense of pride and independence from growing and preserving their own food. What is really important, though, are not the reasons for putting foods by, but the how's and why's of the different processes. We were fortunate in the production of this book to have the talents and first hand experience of Mariel Dewey, an expert in the field of food preservation, and practitioner of many other "lost arts" related to living off the land.

The Dewey family lives on a small working farm near Gilroy, California. Mariel's husband, George, is a farm advisor for the University of California, and Mariel explains she became interested in home economics by helping her husband research many of the questions that came his way. She became more and more interested in the subject and has practically made a career of it by this time.

Many of the projects on the farm in Gilroy were started so that George could have first hand knowledge of the problems other farmers and gardeners were experiencing. Needless-to-say, the more activities there were on the farm, the more agreeably self-sufficient the Dewey's became.

The Dewey's have five children, three of whom are married, practicing the same style of life as they experienced at home. They have one son left at home who Mariel calls an "inveterate animal rescuer" which accounts, in part, for the one hundred

George and Mariel Dewey, and their son Allen. Increased self-sufficiency was the by-product of the many experimental projects conducted on the farm.

and seventy-seven animals kept on the farm (if you count the seventy-four mice).

The animal inventory reads like this: two cats, two dogs, two tortoises, seventy-four mice, seven guinea pigs, one large raccoon, one hawk, one owl, one ram, ten ewes, fifteen lambs, three goats, four kids, three milk cows, two steers, thirty-four ducks, two drakes, ten geese, and three ganders. From the animals, the garden and the 4-H classes, and all the on-going projects, one can tell that the Dewey's farm is a busy place.

Mariel recently taught a class on food preservation in conjunction with a gardening class taught by her husband. Many of the ideas and projects for this book sprang from that class, and we feel that readers would benefit most if they viewed this book as a "home extension course." We have tried to cover as many subjects as possible, and in some cases the reader is advised on where to find more information on a particular subject; it was our idea that the information contained in this book would get you started in the right direction.

◁
Mariel Dewey and one of the Muscovy ducks which wander around the farm in Gilroy, California.

If you don't have a garden

Some ideas on where to go to find what you need.

✔For produce, try the pick-it-yourself farms.

✔Try bulk buying and sharing with friends. Before I learned to make my own cheeses, friends and I would purchase wonderful cheeses from a nearby factory. We realized a huge savings by buying in bulk.

✔Watch for produce trucks parked along the highway.

✔Flea markets sometimes include vegetable markets.

✔If possible buy eggs right from the producer.

✔To stock up on chickens, eggs, and produce, plan a weekend trip to the country. Write to your State Development Commission in the State Capitol Building and ask for a directory of manufacturers and producers for your state and area. Find out if they will sell direct or in quantity to private buyers.

✔Try purchasing fish at the dock from fishermen.

✔Find a source of wild berries or beach plums (found on the seashores of the Northeast).

✔Try swapping surplus vegetables and fruits.

✔Write to a nearby small town Chamber of Commerce and ask where fresh produce is available.

In Northern California there is a most useful map called Sonoma County Farm Trails. It lists a large variety of products from strawberries to turkeys available in the area. People follow the map and stop to buy eggs, vegetables, and fruit and to taste wines. Write: P. O. Box 6043, Santa Rosa, CA 95406. Naturally you save money and insure freshness this way. Perhaps a group of people in your area could encourage the local Chamber of Commerce to develop such a tour or list.

For other sources of good food, try outdoor and indoor farmers' markets. Ask old-timers in your area or read small town papers. Send for a sample copy by writing to "the leading newspaper" in the town you are interested in. You'll get a feel for a new area and can determine if it might be worth a weekend trip.

If you don't have a garden, you don't have to want for farm-fresh vegetables. Roadside stands, and pick-it-yourself fruit and vegetable farms provide a wide harvest for the non-gardener.

Where to find it all

The following section is a general list of sources and ideas and where to find equipment, information, and produce. A more specific list of sources for each subject covered is listed on the first page of each chapter.

Each method of preserving the harvest requires some basic equipment. For the most part these "tools of the trade" last a lifetime and are well worth the original investment. Knowing where to look for these supplies, though, and having luck finding them can be a problem in some areas.

I always try the local stores first; if I am disappointed, a talk to the store manager will sometimes bring good results. If the local sources are unable to fill my needs I consult the mail order houses. I receive many fabulous catalogs each year and have had great luck ordering the supplies by mail. The catalogs alone are well worth reading and studying. The following recommended catalogs are ones which I have found most helpful for both supplies and information. At this writing there are no charges other than noted. Once you order, you remain on their mailing lists for some time.

General catalogs

HAMILTON BOOKS
30 Chambers Road, Danbury, CT 06810
I have ordered many interesting cookbooks and how-to-do-it manuals from Hamilton. They send out free catalogs several times a year.

J. C. PENNEY CO., INC.
1301 Avenue of the Americas
New York, NY 10019
A general catalog, including canning equipment and storage.

MAID OF SCANDINAVIA CO.
3244 Raleigh Avenue
Minneapolis, MN 55416
Send 25¢ for a big catalog of kitchen equipment, decorating supplies, flavorings, and appliances.

MOTHER'S BOOK SHELF
P. O. Box 70
Hendersonville, NC 28739
Books for do-it-yourself, homesteading, and food preservation.

MOTHER'S GENERAL STORE
Box 506, Flat Rock, NC 28731
A most fascinating catalog containing many old fashioned items. One of my very favorite catalogs.

MONTGOMERY WARD
Chicago, IL 60607
Write to the main headquarters and they will likely send a catalog. Ask for the Farm and Garden catalog for wine supplies, milk filters, and other surprising farm aids.

NASCO
901 Janesville, Fort Atkinson, WI 53538
or
1524 Princeton Avenue
Modesto, CA 95382
They have several large, free catalogs, including separate ones for arts and crafts, farm equipment, home economics, and many more.

SEARS, ROEBUCK AND COMPANY
2650 E. Olympic Blvd.
Los Angeles, CA 90051
Write for a sample catalog (e.g., The Farm and Garden catalog). If you make an order, you'll be on their regular mailing list. A secondary mail order address for the East is 4640 Roosevelt Blvd., Philadelphia, PA 19132. Write to the closest address.

WHOLE EARTH ACCESS CO.
2466 Shattuck Ave.
Berkeley, CA 97404
Probably the most complete source we found for any of the equipment, tools, or further information described in this book, with the added bonus of the low list prices on most items. Everything is here, from grain mills to fruit presses, as well as an excellent inventory of reference materials.

State and government publications

Some states have excellent publications either for free or for a small charge. Write to your particular Land Grant University and ask for a list of available publications. Sometimes they will even send photostats of out-of-print publications.

Other mail order book sources

SUPERINTENDENT OF DOCUMENTS
U. S. GOVERNMENT PRINTING OFFICE
Washington, DC 30402
Send 45¢ for this catalog, stock number 0103-0002.

GARDEN WAY PUBLISHERS
Charlotte, VT 05445
Free information on this catalog will be sent upon request. If you order a book, you will be put on the mailing list. I have found books on building presses, cooking, canning, gardening, cheese-making, and other homesteading concepts.

THE GREAT OUTDOORS BOOK LIST
LEON R. GREENMAN, INC.
132 Spring Street, New York, NY 10012
Lists almost every book on nature, mountaincraft, cooking, camping, and travel. A wonderful and complete list.

Cookbooks by mail from:
CORNER BOOK SHOP
102 Fourth Avenue
New York, NY 10003
Second-hand books available from:
STRAND BOOK STORE, INC.
828 Broadway, New York, NY 10003
Ask for a specific subject.

Some fascinating catalogs for kitchen equipment and foods

VERMONT COUNTRY STORE
Weston, VT 05161

BAZAAR DE LA CUISINE INTERNATIONAL
1003 2nd Avenue
New York, NY 10026

BAZAAR FRANÇAIS
666 Sixth Avenue
New York, NY 10010

LEKVAR BY THE BARREL
H. ROTH AND SON
1577 First Avenue
New York, NY 10028

MANGANAROS
488 Ninth Avenue
New York, NY 10018

COLONIAL GARDEN KITCHENS
270 W. Merrick Road
Valley Stream, NY 11582

THE GREAT VALLEY MILLS
Quakertown, PA 18951

PAPRIKAS WEISS
1546 Second Avenue
New York, NY 10026

LES ECHALOTTES
Ramsey, NJ 07446

NICHOLS GARDEN NURSERY
1190 No. Pacific Highway
Albany, OR 97321

CALIFORNIA ALMOND GROWERS EXCHANGE
P. O. Box 1768, Sacramento, CA 95808

YOUNG PECAN SALES CORP.
P. O. Box 632, Florence, SC 29501

NORTHWESTERN COFFEE MILLS STORE
217 N. Broadway, Milwaukee, WI 53202

MERRY GARDENS
Camden, ME 04843

Sure sign of the autumn harvest; an incredible selection of pumpkins near Half Moon Bay, California.

Contact the Extension Agent at your State University Agricultural Department for a list of farm sources for produce. Try special ordering produce from your regular market. Often they will be happy to order an extra lug of fruit for you. Read automobile club magazines for interesting tours.

Wholesale terminals frequently will sell to individuals. Don't be too fussy and be prepared to take a large, unsorted quantity. You may take home some bad with the good, but the price is well worth it. Try the terminals early in the morning for the best produce.

For quantity purchasing, ask a friendly restauranteur for help in finding what you need. Restaurant suppliers frequently carry big crocks, canning size kettles, pressure cookers, and other useful equipment.

There are co-ops throughout the United States for feeds, foods, and farm supplies. Look in the yellow pages of the telephone directory.

Health food stores might be a good source for grains, seeds, and for information regarding produce. For supplies to preserve and smoke meats or color cheese, try the druggist.

Farmers' cooperatives such as the Farm Bureau, Grange, National Farm Organization might provide sources for food, equipment, and information. Try the farmers' supply for equipment not normally carried in department stores. Try nursery and garden supply houses for crocks and barrels.

This is like a game of hide and seek. If you are interested in finding out how to do things, you must be prepared to do a lot of research before you find success. People are usually helpful and will often give you more information than you thought existed. Good luck to you and with patience you'll find what you need.

The rhythm of the harvest

Making the most out of each season is an important part of preserving food; a consultant in California wrote and told us of her rather unique method:

"Few people can afford the time to be totally involved in preserving the harvest for the coming winter. Because I don't always have as much time as I wish I had, I have my own kind of mental calendar for food preservation.

"For early spring it's freezer jam when the strawberries are good; loganberry jam follows soon after when my neighbor's daughter sells her berries. Apricots ripen next and that means drying, jam and chutney.

"We never grow zucchini as I know that, from year to year, friends will give us part of their over-abundance; the zucchini is made into bread, or put up in the freezer.

"Japanese cucumbers come next from another friend, and these are made into pickles. By July 20th, I am looking for an excuse to make a trip up near Sebastopol so I can get 100 pounds of Gravensteins for apple-sauce and the freezer.

"Each August we receive an abundance of wild blackberries and Himalaya berries which my dad picks, along with a great many trout and salmon which I freeze. Labor day, and the figs are plentiful, more than we can eat fresh, resulting in dried figs and jam.

"In mid-September I clean up the tomato vines and make tomato chutney and tomato relish with the green tomatoes. By late September I plan to see a friend in Walnut Creek for the visit as well as to get walnuts, which I crack and shell by the hour. Late October and I finally get a few fruit cakes under way—never as many as planned, though.

"This isn't much of a pattern or rhythm, but it is something I do year in and year out. No matter how busy, I do all of this and try to work in one or two new things each year, as well. My mental clock tells me that we can't take a vacation in late July when the apricots ripen, just as strongly as the fact that we must be back here in time for school in September."

When you have a garden

Planning a garden for seasonal, fresh produce is one thing; planning a garden for a *12-Months Harvest* is something quite different.

In the next chapter we have taken a look at a number of successful gardeners who have *planned* gardens, not only for the fresh produce, but for the long range harvest as well. There's a real knack involved in this type of gardening. These gardeners all agreed on the importance of a well thought out plan coupled with the necessity of keeping a record of local weather conditions from year to year, to achieve the best results.

Through experience, they have become "12-Month Harvesters." By following some of their suggestions, we believe you can do the same, no matter what size garden you have.

As anyone with a garden will tell you—homegrown vegetables aren't necessarily better than the store bought variety—they just taste that way. A full basket during the fall harvest means a full pantry for the rest of the year.

Stretching a 7-months growing season into a 12-months eating season

When you set about planning, planting, and caring for a garden for a 12-months supply of vegetables, you have a job on your hands that's quite different than just growing vegetables.

It calls for more than bringing in a succession of harvests throughout the growing season, in the quantities the family can use. That's difficult enough. But to that skill, you must add the know-how of the right variety at the right time for the storing, freezing, canning departments.

In the following 14 pages we have brought together the experiences of many 12-month gardeners in many different climates. To their experience we have added our own, plus reports from the USDA and its localized Extension Service.

Throughout these pages we have drawn heavily upon the experience of John Bridgman, who gardens in Northern California, and Sid Harkema, who gardens in Grand Rapids, Michigan. Both are exceptionally good record keepers. Measured by growing season—the number of days between the last and first frost—the gardens are similar. But in the Bridgman garden, winter weather does not bring all plant growth to a complete stop as it does in the Harkema garden.

Gardens in low deserts of the Southwest and the deep South are not forgotten. Where "spring planting" starts in October and the fall, winter and early spring is the important growing season, a different emphasis is placed on the 12-month harvest. In the warm winter areas, growing season and not the storing season is the important consideration.

We would like to promise the gardeners who are tackling the job for the first time that in these pages they will find an easy-to-follow guide to a successful 12-month garden. But from our experience—and from the records of many 12-monthers—the first time around is just Experiment No. 1. The best we can do is to shorten the time it takes to work out a successful operation. You can learn by our mistakes.

Here, John Bridgman talks about some of his experiences in arriving at successive plantings, following recommended dates for sowing seed, and other problems.

Successive planting

"Everybody plants too much in the spring and runs out in the summer with respect to many vegetables. Catalogs and most books are unrealistic in their suggestion for succession plantings every 10 days or 2 weeks. It's not that simple, but at the same time, anyone beyond the first year beginner state can arrange to have certain vegetables over a relatively long period of time. The key, however, is good planning and record keeping; quite a lot of paper work, but rewarding.

"Take peas for example. We always start with one row of 'Alaska' because it's too wet and cold in mid-February for the regular varieties. My life is complicated at the moment because we are trying out 'Green Arrow.' It's much simpler to stick with one variety and avoid various maturity spans. We will probably go back to 'Progress' exclusively (plus one planting of 'Alaska'). 'Green Arrow' is a great pea but it takes 10-14 days longer to mature in our garden.

"The point is that a succession of picking dates can be arrived at only after experimental plantings have given you the actual growing time related to time of planting in your own garden. After 3 years of record keeping I can adjust the published maturity span to the actual span and get the succession of crops I want."

Variety	Plant	Days to maturity claimed	Days to maturity actual	Due date
Alaska	2/10	55	80	May 1
Progress	2/10	60	85	May 6
Progress	3/2	60	75	May 16
Green Arrow	3/2	70	90	May 31
Progress	3/16	60	70	May 25
Green Arrow	3/16	70	85	June 9
Progress	4/20	60	60	June 19
Green Arrow	4/20	70	70	June 29

As the chart shows, the record will be continued. The due date will vary from the actual date according to the weather, but the rhythm of the harvest will follow the same sequence.

Starting from transplants

"Raising seedlings at home for transplanting is more difficult and troublesome than some books would indicate. Much as I love gardening, I have to admit that nursery-grown seedlings are *at least* as high in quality to any I can grow myself, and well worth the price when only small quantities are involved.

"Nevertheless, there are two occasions when raising your own transplants is imperative and very reward-

Top: In the Harkema garden, in Grand Rapids, Michigan, close spacing, fast succession of crops, and soil storage through the winter make it a most successful 12-month garden.
Bottom: In the Hojinacki garden, also in Grand Rapids, where a lawn gave way to an extensive vegetable garden, at the same time maintaining the green carpet feel of the lawn.

ing. The first is when you want a hard-to-find variety; the second is a matter of timing. In general, the nurseries offer seedlings at typical planting times—raising your own is a great advantage if, (a) you are trying to beat the season or extend it, or (b) you want to plant a vegetable in succession, after the nurseries no longer offer it. For example, I like to plant six or so cabbages every two weeks from February into mid-summer, so I usually have a small seed bed just for raising cabbage seedlings to facilitate the succession plantings.''

Spring planting dates

''All calendars don't agree—they can't when it comes to local planting dates and days to maturity. My neighbor's are two to three weeks ahead of me in the spring, and their garden is only a mile away from ours, but at a higher elevation (cold air settles in our pocket). This means that any gardener beyond the rank beginner stage has to learn his temperature and frost conditions and work out his own planting schedules.

''Each year I get 'antsy' and try to beat the season, and each year the earliest plantings fail to mature significantly ahead of the vegetables planted at the appropriate time—this is true even later in spring. For a few years I grew squash in peat pots indoors and planted in the garden around the 10th of May, but they stood still for a couple of weeks, so I quit the practice and now plant seeds directly into hills after the last frost (around May 15).''

Mid-summer planting for late fall harvest

''Our best bet for a late fall harvest is our third beet crop ('Detroit Dark Red') planted —June 15, our third carrot crop ('Red Cored Chantenay') planted June 20, our later successive plantings of 'Morden Dwarf' cabbage from seed (we sow enough seeds for 6-10 cabbages about once a month from spring well into summer), and onions which we plant from sets ('White Pearl') around August 1, which make entirely adequate green onions for a fall harvest.''

Black plastic mulch

The enthusiasm of the users of black plastic is contagious. Last year when we were working on the book *Gardening Shortcuts,* we checked out the experience of Gus Gagis, of Wayne, New Jersey, with his black plastic garden. (See page 27 of Gardening Shortcuts.) Was his experiment successful? A follow-up this year finds Gus increasing the size of his garden and the black plastic mulch.

The benefits of black plastic is enthusiastically supported in this letter from Robert Rusk, of Rockville, Maryland. We quote:

''This is my third season of gardening. The first year I had just bought this house and had no time to do anything but throw some seeds and tomato transplants at the ground. I got some tomatoes and squash mixed in with the weeds. Last year I did my gardening with "All About Vegetables" in one figurative hand, and seeds in the other, and got very good results.

''This will be the second year I've laid 4-mil black plastic in 10' x 25' sheets wall-to-wall. I second the comments of Gus Gagis in "Garden-

An early start and a late finish

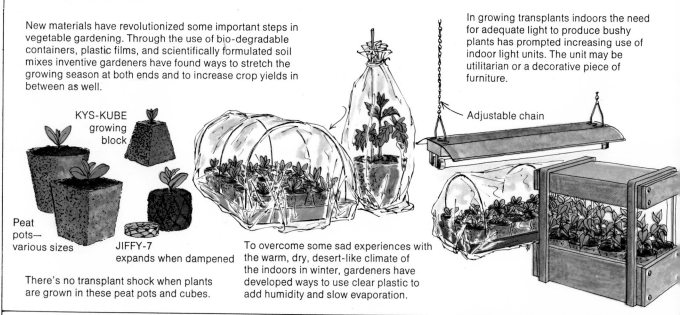

New materials have revolutionized some important steps in vegetable gardening. Through the use of bio-degradable containers, plastic films, and scientifically formulated soil mixes inventive gardeners have found ways to stretch the growing season at both ends and to increase crop yields in between as well.

KYS-KUBE growing block

Peat pots—various sizes

JIFFY-7 expands when dampened

There's no transplant shock when plants are grown in these peat pots and cubes.

To overcome some sad experiences with the warm, dry, desert-like climate of the indoors in winter, gardeners have developed ways to use clear plastic to add humidity and slow evaporation.

In growing transplants indoors the need for adequate light to produce bushy plants has prompted increasing use of indoor light units. The unit may be utilitarian or a decorative piece of furniture.

Adjustable chain

The bio-degradable container has encouraged gardeners to grow transplants of many plants that were formerly direct seeded—beans, squash, cucumbers, and melons for example. But, the root crops—carrots, salsify, parsnips, etc.—are better sown in place. When germinating these seeds outdoors you have two stumbling blocks to overcome. The drying of the soil and the crusting

of the soil surface. Clear plastic, laid over the row after sowing does both, as well as speeding up germination. Remove as soon as seedlings emerge.

Hold edges with soil

Planter mix

Seeds

Replacing the garden soil in the row with planter mix does a nice job, too—and it provides for good root development

ing Shortcuts." It does look silly early in the season, but once it grows leaves, stand back cause it's gonna grow faster than you can back-pedal. Besides increasing yields per square foot compared to other local gardens, it runs productivity in terms of vegetables per man hour, right through the ceiling.

"Unfortunately, like so many good ideas, it is expensive at $5 something for 250 square feet. I left it on the ground all winter, and found it unusable in spring. This year I'm going to take every precaution to see if I can't use it again next year."

Black polyethylene film has earned the affection of the commercial vegetable grower as well as the home gardener for the production of warm weather crops—especially melons, squash, and peppers.

The use of drip irrigation systems, with the tubing laid beneath the plastic mulch, has solved the irrigation problem for commercial growers.

The home gardener takes care of irrigation needs in many ways. Home garden drip irrigation kits (such as Viaflow and DripEze) are becoming more available. Some gardeners use the old time soaker hose beneath the plastic. Those using sprinkler irrigation, or those depending on rain for a portion of the water requirement, cut slits or inverted T's in the plastic film.

In our use of black plastic we lay down strips of 3 foot wide plastic film with 3 feet open soil between the strips. The planting bed is slightly mounded—higher than the soil between the plastic. Transplants of bush summer and winter squash, tomatoes, peppers, and eggplant are set in single rows in the center of the plastic strips. Wire cages for training tomatoes are set in the plastic. Pole beans are set out in double rows near each edge of the plastic and trained as they grow to a single trellis. When plantings are underway the space between the plastic is mulched with sawdust or ground bark.

And what have I got? The black plastic speeds early growth due to slightly warmer soil and lack of weed competition. As the weather warms and plants grow their leaves shade the plastic. The plastic slows down moisture loss. Because there is no chopping hoe to remove weeds the plant roots work in the rich top inches of the soil. The swing of day and night soil temperatures is less under the plastic film than in the open ground.

The organic mulch between the plastic strip gives a mud-free path at all times. Water from the sky or sprinkler penetrates through it.

Why not an organic mulch throughout the garden? In early spring nothing should stop the sun's rays from warming the soil. Organic mulches—straw, bark, or whatever should be applied *after* the soil warms.

The imperfect green world

In a perfect world, planning is a matter of simple arithmetic. If you are starting tomato plants in a temperature controlled greenhouse, you know that the first true leaves are open about 3 weeks from sowing. In 6 to 8 weeks from sowing, plants will be the right size for transplanting. Experience tells you that normally,

Protection from frost, wind, animals, and birds is illustrated in the photo panels on the following pages.
In both the early start and the late finish the values of the raised-bed method of growing vegetables cannot be stressed too much. If the soil within the bed drains well it will warm up earlier in the spring and crops will come faster than those in surrounding soils.

Plastic film over wood or wire-mesh structure

Frost protection, hail and heavy rain protection is easier to arrange in raised beds

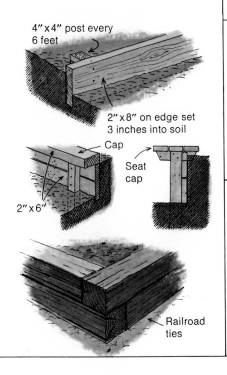

4" x 4" post every 6 feet

2" x 8" on edge set 3 inches into soil

Cap

Seat cap

2" x 6"

Railroad ties

High water-table or waterlogged soil makes fall and winter storage of root crops and potatoes hazardous—causes rot. If you don't wish to go to the trouble of raised beds of wood, arrange raised beds of soil and get drainage by ditching.

Drainage ditch

Winter protection

Summer shade

And don't forget, one of the oldest gardening aids in the history of gardening—the cold frame.

the temperature outdoors in your garden is right on about April 20 or May 20, or whatever date the nights are about 55° (at least in the first 4 hours of darkness—and the soil is warm). So, you figure back 6 to 8 weeks and sow the seed about February 20 or March 20. But April 20 or May 20 and the 15 days following turn out to be abnormally cold—a record breaking last frost hits the garden. Meanwhile the transplants grow too tall, become rootbound, harden. So you hesitate. Should you plant and protect, or move the transplants into large containers and grow them on?

When growing plants indoors it's easy to think that you are going to get the jump on the season by sowing seed early. But you soon find out that a seedling of pepper or eggplant ready to transplant in late April won't have a place in the garden until late May or early June.

In planning a garden you start transplants to arrive at planting size on a date favorable to their continued growth. The number of weeks needed to grow to transplant size is known. The optimum planting date is a moving target. The date of the last frost in your garden varies from year to year, and the cool spring may linger for weeks or rush into summer overnight.

The record-keeping 12-monther has the best chance of hitting the optimum planting date with the right sized transplant.

One figure on the time it takes to grow from seed to transplant size is given in the statistics on each vegetable discussed in the last six pages of this chapter. But you will note that they are elastic figures. The time varies according to light and temperature.

Greenhouse growing

In the wholesale catalog of Geo. Ball, Inc.—a respected authority in greenhouse and bedding plant operations—the commercial grower of vegetables is informed of each vegetable's growing requirement. (Note: In your growing from seed to transplant size, you may not enjoy the luxury of controlled temperatures. However, the grower experience is a good guide to approximate on window sills, under lights, or whatever.)

The catalog goes like this:

Beets: Seed 3-4 weeks from sowing. Can be germinated (15 days) and grown cool, 50°-70°. Set out very early in spring, successively through June and again in fall.

Broccoli: Sell 4-6 weeks from sowing. Germinate (10 days) at 70°, and grow cool 60°. Offer plants for sale in spring and in July for fall gardening.

Brussels Sprouts: Saleable when 4-6 weeks old. Germinate (10 days) at 70°, and grow cool 60°. Set out in early spring and mid-July for fall harvest.

Cabbage: Grow seedlings 3-4 weeks at 60° and harden one week for sales. Germinate (10 days) at 70°. Sell early in spring.

Cauliflower: Plants should be sold young 4-5 weeks old. Germinate (10 days) at 70°. Grow cool, 60°, after germination. Offer in spring for late April planting or in late July for fall harvest.

Celery: Saleable 8-10 weeks from sowing. Cover seeds, keep moist and

More about protection—early and late

Inventive gardeners find ways of stretching the harvest by advancing spring and prolonging fall, but there's more to the job than providing extra warmth. **1.** *A portable A-frame is converted into early season protection for tomatoes by using plastic. Black plastic is also used as a mulch here. Experimental use of plastic jugs filled with water; sun's rays heat water during the day—the jugs, in turn, radiate warmth during the night.* **2.** *Simple row cover for frost protection made with wire hoops and clear plastic.* **3-4.** *Wire covered frame, used to protect plantings from birds, doubles as row tent with the addition of clear plastic over the wire.*

germinate (10-21 days) at 70°. After germination grow cool, 60°.

Cucumber: Saleable plants in 3-5 weeks. Germinate (7 days) at 80°.

Eggplant: Saleable in 6-8 weeks. Requires warm soil for germination, 80°. Grow seedling 62° nights, 70° days.

Lettuce: Saleable in 4-5 weeks. Germinate at 70° (7 days). Grow plants cool, 55°-60°. For early spring, late fall plant sales.

Melon (cantaloupe): Grow saleable plants 3-5 weeks, short growing season, 5 weeks. Germinate (10 days) at 80°.

Onions: Saleable 6-8 weeks minimum. Germinate (10 days) at 70°, grow 55° nights.

Peppers: Saleable plants 6-8 weeks. Need warm temperature for germination 80° (10 days). Grow seedlings at 62° nights, 70° days. Set plants out well after last frost.

Pumpkin: Saleable in 3-5 weeks. Germinate (7 days) warm, 80°.

Squash: Saleable 3-5 weeks. Germinates (7 days) warm, 80°.

Tomatoes: Plants can be sold 6-8 weeks. Germinate (7-14 days) warm, 80°.

Watermelon: Saleable in 3-5 weeks. Germinate (10 days) warm, 80°. Northern areas grow watermelon when started indoors.

The second spring

Gardeners run on a special time clock. There is an inner hunger to join in the rush of spring. The natural urge to plant the first comfortable days outdoors. Then there is a spell come July or August, when weeding, watering, and seemingly endless picking takes some of the enthusiasm out of gardening. Good gardeners can become tired of gardening. Rejuvenation of the gardening spirit comes with the breaking of the summer heat and the cooler days of early fall.

The production-minded gardener can't run on that time clock. To get a fall harvest, certain planting dates must be met in July and August, when the urge to plant is not in the heart. See the following planning charts for the 12-monthers' planting dates.

The Harkema garden

The Sid Harkema family in Grand Rapids, Michigan grow a lot of vegetables; last year, in fact, over 4000 pounds of fresh vegetables. The only vegetables Betsy Harkema had to buy last year were a few heads of lettuce in the middle of winter. What makes this garden different, though, is not the tremendous production, but the methods the Harkemas use to get that production from a 45 by 75 foot garden space.

Sid told us: "I have a family of 5 children and since they help grow the vegetables they are also crazy about eating them. Every year we try some new varieties as well as our old stand-bys. All of this takes a lot of space—more space than I have." The high productivity, according to Sid, is the result of a planned succession of crops—never one square foot of idle ground—optimum planting dates, maximum use of space, and a careful choice of varieties.

"Succession of crops appears simple on paper. In the garden it becomes complicated when spacing of the crops differ in widths such as

1. *When the sun is boiling hot, sunburn is a hazard with many fruits, especially melons. Here, gardener has built small shade houses for melon protection. Some commercial growers whitewash melons if they are without leaf cover and exposed to direct sun.* **2-3-4.** *Vegetables cannot make normal growth and protect themselves from the wind at the same time. In addition to possible wind breakage, the plant is stunted because the leaves will close up shop or wilt with excessive air movement. Young transplants are especially susceptible to wind damage.* **5.** *Fall rains can put an end to the tomato season; here a tomato-wise gardener drapes plastic film over tomatoes in wire cages and adds a month to his tomato harvest. Plastic cover of this type is safe in cool, rainy fall weather. However, when using clear plastic for early-season protection, watch out for sudden changes in weather, heat builds up rapidly under clear plastic in full sun. Provide ventilation, air circulation to prevent burning plants.*

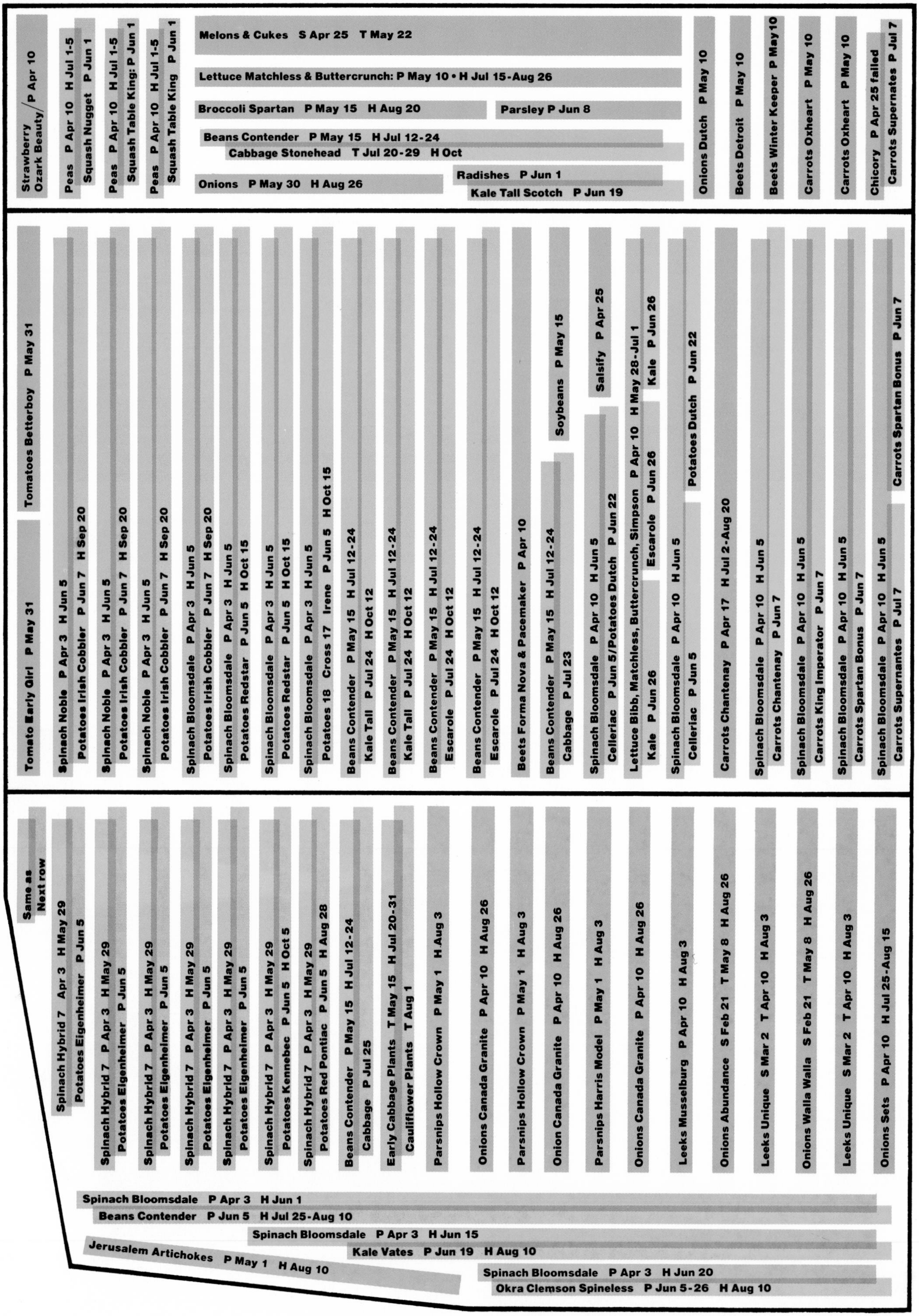

Top section

- Strawberry Ozark Beauty / P Apr 10
- Peas P Apr 10 H Jul 1-5
- Squash Nugget P Jun 1
- Peas P Apr 10 H Jul 1-5
- Squash Table King: P Jun 1
- Peas P Apr 10 H Jul 1-5
- Squash Table King P Jun 1
- Melons & Cukes S Apr 25 T May 22
- Lettuce Matchless & Buttercrunch: P May 10 • H Jul 15-Aug 26
- Broccoli Spartan P May 15 H Aug 20
- Parsley P Jun 8
- Beans Contender P May 15 H Jul 12-24
- Cabbage Stonehead T Jul 20-29 H Oct
- Onions P May 30 H Aug 26
- Radishes P Jun 1
- Kale Tall Scotch P Jun 19
- Onions Dutch P May 10
- Beets Detroit P May 10
- Beets Winter Keeper P May 10
- Carrots Oxheart P May 10
- Carrots Oxheart P May 10
- Chicory P Apr 25 failed
- Carrots Supernates P Jul 7

Middle section

- Tomato Early Girl P May 31
- Tomatoes Betterboy P May 31
- Spinach Noble P Apr 3 H Jun 5
- Potatoes Irish Cobbler P Jun 7 H Sep 20
- Spinach Noble P Apr 3 H Jun 5
- Potatoes Irish Cobbler P Jun 7 H Sep 20
- Spinach Noble P Apr 3 H Jun 5
- Potatoes Irish Cobbler P Jun 7 H Sep 20
- Spinach Bloomsdale P Apr 3 H Jun 5
- Potatoes Irish Cobbler P Jun 7 H Sep 20
- Spinach Bloomsdale P Apr 3 H Jun 5
- Potatoes Redstar P Jun 5 H Oct 15
- Spinach Bloomsdale P Apr 3 H Jun 5
- Potatoes Redstar P Jun 5 H Oct 15
- Spinach Bloomsdale P Apr 3 H Jun 5
- Potatoes 18 Cross 17 Irene P Jun 5 H Oct 15
- Beans Contender P May 15 H Jul 12-24
- Kale Tall P Jul 24 H Oct 12
- Beans Contender P May 15 H Jul 12-24
- Kale Tall P Jul 24 H Oct 12
- Beans Contender P May 15 H Jul 12-24
- Escarole P Jul 24 H Oct 12
- Beans Contender P May 15 H Jul 12-24
- Escarole P Jul 24 H Oct 12
- Beets Forma Nova & Pacemaker P Apr 10
- Beans Contender P May 15 H Jul 12-24
- Cabbage P Jul 23
- Soybeans P May 15
- Spinach Bloomsdale P Apr 10 H Jun 5
- Salsify P Apr 25
- Celleriac P Jun 5/Potatoes Dutch P Jun 22
- Lettuce Bibb, Matchless, Buttercrunch, Simpson P Apr 10 H May 28-Jul 1
- Kale P Jun 26
- Escarole P Jun 26
- Kale P Jun 26
- Spinach Bloomsdale P Apr 10 H Jun 5
- Celleriac P Jun 5
- Potatoes Dutch P Jun 22
- Carrots Chantenay P Apr 17 H Jul 2-Aug 20
- Spinach Bloomsdale P Apr 10 H Jun 5
- Carrots Chantenay P Jun 7
- Spinach Bloomsdale P Apr 10 H Jun 5
- Carrots King Imperator P Jun 7
- Spinach Bloomsdale P Apr 10 H Jun 5
- Carrots Spartan Bonus P Jun 7
- Carrots Spartan Bonus P Jun 7
- Spinach Bloomsdale P Apr 10 H Jun 5
- Carrots Supernantes P Jul 7

Bottom section

- Same as Next row
- Spinach Hybrid 7 P Apr 3 H May 29
- Potatoes Eigenheimer P Jun 5
- Spinach Hybrid 7 P Apr 3 H May 29
- Potatoes Eigenheimer P Jun 5
- Spinach Hybrid 7 P Apr 3 H May 29
- Potatoes Eigenheimer P Jun 5
- Spinach Hybrid 7 P Apr 3 H May 29
- Potatoes Eigenheimer P Jun 5
- Spinach Hybrid 7 P Apr 3 H May 29
- Potatoes Eigenheimer P Jun 5
- Spinach Hybrid 7 P Apr 3 H May 29
- Potatoes Kennebec P Jun 5 H Oct 5
- Spinach Hybrid 7 P Apr 3 H May 29
- Potatoes Red Pontiac P Jun 5 H Aug 28
- Beans Contender P May 15 H Jul 12-24
- Cabbage P Jul 25
- Early Cabbage Plants T May 15 H Jul 20-31
- Cauliflower Plants T Aug 1
- Parsnips Hollow Crown P May 1 H Aug 3
- Onions Canada Granite P Apr 10 H Aug 26
- Parsnips Hollow Crown P May 1 H Aug 3
- Onion Canada Granite P Apr 10 H Aug 26
- Parsnips Harris Model P May 1 H Aug 3
- Onions Canada Granite P Apr 10 H Aug 26
- Leeks Musselburg P Apr 10 H Aug 3
- Onions Abundance S Feb 21 T May 8 H Aug 26
- Leeks Unique S Mar 2 T Apr 10 H Aug 3
- Onions Walla Walla S Feb 21 T May 8 H Aug 26
- Leeks Unique S Mar 2 T Apr 10 H Aug 3
- Onions Sets P Apr 10 H Jul 25-Aug 15

Bottom horizontal bars

- Spinach Bloomsdale P Apr 3 H Jun 1
- Beans Contender P Jun 5 H Jul 25-Aug 10
- Spinach Bloomsdale P Apr 3 H Jun 15
- Kale Vates P Jun 19 H Aug 10
- Jerusalem Artichokes P May 1 H Aug 10
- Spinach Bloomsdale P Apr 3 H Jun 20
- Okra Clemson Spineless P Jun 5-26 H Aug 10

when lettuce is followed by cabbage or potatoes."

Sid gets around that difficulty this way: "The rows in the garden are all 2 feet apart, and are permanently marked off on the railroad ties

"I know that some crops require more than 24 inches of space, but by spacing them farther apart within the row I can usually make do. With the 2-foot wide beds throughout, all crops are interchangeable. When the time comes to follow one crop with another I can plug in any type of crop.

Key to garden plan on page 14

The portion of the garden shown is 45 feet wide by 65 feet long.

For ease in planning, all rows are laid out 2 feet apart. Crops like beets and parsnips are sometimes doubled up in actual planting.

Only planting	Long-season crops, only one planting in the row
1st planting / **2nd planting**	Succession planting, both crops in the same row

S = Seeds started indoors
T = Transplants set in the row
P = Seeds planted directly in the row
H = Harvested

"To make maximum use of space, all carrots, radishes, beets, parsnips, onions and the like are planted in double rows within the 2-foot space. Crops that should be planted in rows 30 to 36 inches apart are spaced further apart within the row.

"In some cases I will try to get 3 crops out of the same piece of ground. For example, an early crop of spinach comes off in June. It is followed with potatoes. Before the potatoes are harvested, a planting of kale goes between the potatoes which is harvested before the kale is mature.

"This close spacing has more advantages than increasing production. With the foliage of all plants touching, there's a canopy above the soil. The need for weeding and hoeing is lessened. The foliage also acts as a mulch; the vegetable garden becomes a thing of beauty."

Sid prepares for the unusual frost, early and late, with all kinds of frost protection. What does he use? "Plastic sheets, burlap, blankets, anything that's handy. Individual plant covers, 20-gallon garbage cans for super-early tomatoes, bushel baskets, pails, pots, and irrigation.

Delaware plan

The more conventional plan for succession, as shown below, is not as productive per square foot of space as the Harkema plan. However, if you have the space it is an easier plan to follow or to adapt to your personal scheme.

Blind faith

When you talk of yields per 100 feet of row or days from seed to maturity or any specific measurement as we do in the following pages, you want to add a big "maybe." We want to repeat what was said in *All About Vegetables:*

"Challenge the authorities:

"Don't accept the recipes and directions in this book or any other with blind faith. Only the plants in your garden can tell you the truth and the plant is always right, no matter what an authority has said. Dr. Frits Went says it this way:

" 'Once the amateur has realized that he himself is master of the situation in his garden, and that he is not the slave of a set of recipes, a great deal is gained. Gardening comes

A typical garden calendar

You can plan the succession planting and harvest in your garden by making a calendar like this of your area. This one is for the Delaware area taken from the University of Delaware Extension Service Bulletin 55.

Plant | **Harvest**

Crop	Mar	Apr	May	Jun	July	Aug	Sep	Oct	Nov
Snap beans			Plant→Harvest						
Lima beans			Plant→Harvest						
Cabbage	Plant→Harvest			Plant→Harvest			Harvest		
Cucumbers			Plant→Harvest						
Carrots	Plant→Harvest			Plant→Harvest			Harvest		
Beets	Plant→Harvest			Plant→Harvest			Harvest		
Broccoli					Plant→Harvest		Harvest		
Cauliflower					Plant→Harvest		Harvest		
Cantalope			Plant→Harvest		Harvest				
Lettuce	Plant→Harvest				Harvest		Harvest		
Onions	Plant		Green Onions		Harvest				
Peas	Plant		Peas Harvest						
Peppers			Plant→Harvest		Harvest				
Radish	Plant→Harvest	Plant→Harvest				Harvest	Harvest		
Spinach	Plant→Harvest		Plant→Harvest			Harvest	Harvest		
Sweet Corn			Plant→Harvest		Harvest				
Squash			Plant→Harvest	Harvest					
Winter Squash			Plant→Harvest				Harvest		
Tomatoes			Plant→Harvest		Harvest				
Turnips	Plant			Turnips	Turnips			Turnips	
Watermelon			Plant→Harvest		Harvest				

out of the realm of mystic beliefs, and becomes an adventure in adaptation. Each plant grown becomes an experiment, instead of a routine performance. That plant becomes the test whether the applied principle was right. If the plant does not grow well or dies, the application of the principles was not right, or the conditions were such that the principle did not work. If, on the other hand, the plant behaves well, it shows the applicability of the principle.' ''

''By looking at the plants in this way, a garden becomes immensely interesting, it becomes the testing ground of ideas, and it frees the mind from dogmatism. The gardener becomes aware of the fact that experiments can be carried out everywhere and are not restricted to highly specialized laboratories.

''Science is not a cult, it flourishes where these observations are faithfully recorded.''

How much

In the following pages we bring together a number of statistics useful in planning for the 12-month harvest.

One rather subjective and suspect figure is the amount to ''plant per person.'' This certainly is in the ''who-says-so'' class. We gathered together figures from charts developed by various state universities, As you would guess, the authors of this measurement seldom agreed. We consider these estimates worth publishing on the chance the reader might consider including some of the vegetables the general public has overlooked. Salsify, celeriac, parsnips, Hamburg parsley are in this class.

The many uses of large mesh wire

A reader of some previous ORTHO BOOKS, Robert V. Rusk of Rockville, Md., wrote us to pass on these uses of, ''a material that is nearly as useful as black plastic mulch.'' He uses 6''x6'' concrete reinforcing wire, but large mesh fencing wire works well, too—and it doesn't rust.

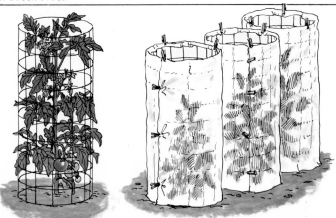

''I grow tomatoes in a cylinder made of a 5'x5' piece, one healthy plant to a cage.''

''I put clear plastic on such cages with clothespins and put them around most anything to greenhouse them early and late in the season.''

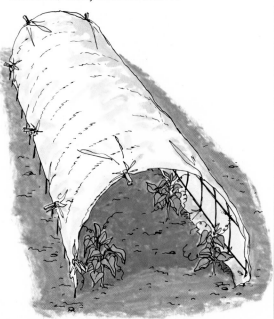

''For row crops I use a half-cylinder lying down, with the points stuck through (the plastic) on one side, and drape the plastic over to the other side where it's held on with clothespins. That way I can fold the stuff back when it's warm, and throw it back over easily when it's cool . . .''

''use it to hold the black plastic down . . . hold your mulches in place with it so the wind doesn't get them.''

''Try doing that with peas, and then let the peas climb the wire as they grow.''

''Rot your leaves in it . . .''

''The combination of black plastic on the bottom and clear plastic overhead really generates and stores some heat!''

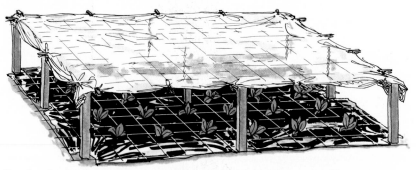

''. . . I understand you can even use it for making things with concrete!''

If you garden with food production and storage as your goal, there's the prejudiced palate as a handicap. Learn to eat what you grow, might be your motto. Gardening (and a good cook) changes vegetable eating habits.

Sid Harkema talks of his experience with beets: "One of the easiest things to grow. The family despised these things the first time they ate them. Because they are so easy to grow and because they are so productive, we just kept on eating them until we liked them. Now everybody loves them. The variety we grow is 'Formanova,' a long, slender English type beet, very nice for slicing and canning. Another is 'Detroit Dark Red.' From this 30-foot row we have harvested 50 pounds with about another 75 pounds to come this year."

One vegetable that is not included in our discussion of individual vegetables is the Jerusalem artichoke—which has nothing to do with Jerusalem, nor is it related to the artichoke. It's a tuberous rooted sunflower—a North American native. Start with a tuber or two and you will have a hundred. Tubers can be left in the ground over winter. No insects or disease trouble it. No one who plants Jerusalem artichoke will ever starve. It's a foolproof food producer.

It may be prepared in all ways that potatoes are served, and more. We like it raw or used lightly salted in salads, or sliced and sautéed in butter, just until tender.

Risk

As you can see in all suggestions offered the 12-monthers in winter cold areas, plantings for fall and winter harvests are restricted to the cool-weather vegetables. Most of them are benefited by a good frost.

How about the gardener who is willing to gamble on the first frost date of fall and plant an extra late crop of sweet corn or beans; to him, one win is worth two losses. Dealing with a fall frost that varies as much as 30 days encourages the gambling spirit. In one of our test gardens the weather bureau says that October 30 is our normal first frost date. Last year we bet that it would be later and with an August 15 planting we could enjoy fresh corn and snap beans for Thanksgiving. We picked corn on that holiday and into December. We will plant a late crop again this year. Perhaps stagger the plantings to reduce the risk.

Ground storage

Sid Harkema has his way of storing root crops so that they can be harvested fresh from the garden throughout the winter months. Sid reports: "Letting mother nature store vegetables year round is no new trick. The pioneers had to depend on this method in order to have a winter and spring supply of food. Come late October, when winter sets into Michigan, we have an ample supply of carrots, leeks, onions, kale, Jerusalem artichokes, and parsnips left in the ground to see us through to next year's first harvest. The vegetables don't grow during the winter months but with a few inches of mulch to keep the ground from freezing, the crop will be kept fresh and can be harvested as needed."

1. *Winter view of the Harkema garden. See Page 8 for its summer look.*
2. *All vegetables are given straw mulch protection. Here leeks are exposed.*
3. *When Jerusalem artichokes are on the menu, they are ready fresh from the snow.* 4. *A fresh harvest of winter vegetables are hosed off on the patio.*

What, where, how much...

Here and in the following five pages we note some of the particulars the 12-month gardener must consider. What vegetables can be stored and where. How much to plant. How long will the vegetable occupy the soil. Statistics given on what, where, and how much, are generalizations and must be adjusted to individual eating habits, size of garden, variations in seasonal weather, local garden environment, and intentions of storing, freezing, canning, etc.

We assume that you are a *successful* grower of vegetables. We do not attempt to condense our book, *All About Vegetables,* to these few pages. Using a selected list of vegetables, we attempt to add to the know-how of the gardener who plans to stretch a 6-month growing season into a 12-month eating season.

Note: Quotes from our recording gardeners are credited to the individual following the quote with his initials. JB is John Bridgman; SH is Sid Harkema.

Asparagus

The seemingly long delay in getting the first crop of this productive vegetable frightens many a gardener from establishing it. However, a few plants in a corner of the garden will produce generously year after year.

* *From seed to harvest: 3 years*
* *From plants (crowns): Buy 1 year old crowns and save a year*
* *Plants per 100 feet: 70 crowns*
* *Yield per 100 feet of row: 30-40 pounds*
* *Plants per person: 10-30 crowns*

Let the plant produce "fern" — removing no shoots the year the plants are set out. Keep the cutting period short the second year. The third year should give you four weeks of cutting. Shoots that grow to "fern" stage in the fall will renew the roots.

Choose the resistant varieties — 'Mary Washington' or 'Waltham Washington.'

Bean (Snap)

The choice between planting bush beans and pole beans goes like this: those who favor bush beans are happy about avoiding setting poles or building trellises. Those who favor pole beans (generally gardeners with limited space) point out the heavier production over a longer period with beans on trellis, teepee, string or fence.

Whether you grow bush or pole beans, remember that snap beans should be picked before they are mature and large seeds develop. A few old pods left on the vine will reduce the set of new ones.

* *Days to germination: 6 to 10*
* *Days from seed to harvest: Bush — 50 to 65*
  Pole — 60 to 70
* *Planting per person: Bush — 20 to 40 feet*
  Pole — 10 to 15 feet
* *Plants per 100 foot row: Bush — 1 pound seed*
  Pole — ½ pound seed
* *Yield per 100 foot row: Bush — 50 pounds*
  Pole — 60 pounds

High temperatures (above 90°) cause poor pod set.

Lack of moisture in the soil will cause plant to produce deformed pods — "polywogs."

In the Harkema Garden: "We plant a few feet of bean row every two weeks for fresh use. But the crop to be canned totals 150 feet and is planted May 1. The harvest is concentrated. We pick four crops, four or five days apart and then we are done."

Beets

Cool weather crop. Poor quality when grown in hot weather.

In mild summer areas make successive sowings at intervals of about 3 weeks in order to have a continuous supply of young, tender beets throughout the season.

* *Days to germination: 7 to 10*
* *Days from seed to harvest: 55 to 65*
* *Plants per 100 feet: 2 ounces of seed*
* *Yield per 100 feet of row: 80 pounds*
* *Plants per person: 5 to 10 feet*

For use during growing season these are representative varieties: 'Ruby Queen' (54 days), 'Burpee Golden' (55 days), 'Detroit Dark Red' (60 days).

For storage the variety 'Long Season' or 'Winter Keeper' gets the nod. "The beets will grow to ¾ the size of your head — quite unbelievable — and remain sweet and non-fibrous right into spring. We plant about 35 feet around July 20. It is most important to keep thinning these beets so that their growth is not checked. Eventually they have to be 6 to 8 inches apart." (JB)

When lifting, great care must be taken to ensure that the roots are not in any way damaged for with many varieties, the smallest cut or bruising of the skin will cause the roots to "bleed" so that when pickled they will turn pink and will have lost much flavor.

Broccoli

Best as a fall/winter crop or planted in very early spring.

* *Days to germination: 3 to 10*
* *Weeks to transplant size: 5 to 7*
* *Days from transplant to harvest: 60 to 80*
* *Plantings per person: 5 to 10 plants or 10 feet of row*
* *Plants per 100 feet of row: ¼ ounce of seed, or 80 plants*
* *Yield per 100 feet of row: 50 to 60 head*

For early plantings: 'Green Comet' (40 days), 'Premium Crop' (58 days) single head, outstanding holding ability.

For fall-winter harvests: 'Waltham 29' (74 days).

Brussels Sprouts

Fresh from the garden it has more delicate flavor than store bought. One of the hardiest vegetables. Plant for winter harvest. Brussels sprouts dislike summer heat.

* *Days to germination: 3 to 10*
* *Weeks to transplant size: 4 to 6*
* *Days from seed to harvest: 110 to 120*
* *Days from transplant to harvest: 80 to 90*
* *Planting per person: 10 feet*
* *Plants per 100 feet of row: 65 plants or 1 packet of seed*
* *Yield per 100 feet of row: 60 pounds or 100 quarts*

In the late fall or early winter the leaves can be removed from the stalk and the whole stalk with its sprouts can be hung in a cool dry cellar for late winter use.

Cabbage

A cool weather crop, the heads of early varieties split soon after they mature in warm weather. To slow up splitting, partially root prune the plants or twist the plant to break some of the roots.

* *Days to germination: 3 to 10*
* *Weeks to transplant size: 5 to 7*
* *Days from transplant to harvest: 65 to 95*
* *Days from seed to harvest: 90 to 150*
* *Planting per person: 3 to 5 plants for early varieties*
  8 plants for late varieties

- *Plants per 100 feet of row: 1 packet or ¼ ounce*
- *Yield per 100 feet of row: 100 to 175 pounds*

Of the early varieties these are All America Selections: 'Ruby Ball' (68 days), 'Stonehead' (70 days).

Late varieties are the good keepers: 'Danish Ballhead' (110 days), 'Chieftain Savoy' (88 days); its crinkled and deeply veined leaves enable winter rains to drain away quickly so that the heart never becomes wet and soggy.

"For winter we planted seed of the 'Danish Ballhead' on June 29 and transplanted 35 seedlings on July 20. We have found that they are one of the better keepers in storage." (JB)

Carrots

An important vegetable in the 12-month garden. Heavy production throughout the growing season. Hardy, can be started in the soil or in sand. Freezes well. Growing in raised beds filled with specially prepared light soil reduces cracking and disease problems from excess water in the fall. Soil warms up earlier in raised beds than the regular garden soil can be worked. Digging is no trouble in raised beds.

- *Days to germination: 10 to 17*
- *Days from seed to harvest: 60 to 80*
- *Planting per person: 30 to 40 feet*
- *Plants per 100 feet of row: ¾ ounce of seed*
- *Yield per 100 feet of row: 75 to 125 pounds or 30 to 50 dozen*

Many varieties. If you have preference for young carrots, make several sowings from spring to mid-summer. There are short ones and long ones. 'Little Finger' and 'Short 'n Sweet' are 3 to 4 inches long. 'Nantes,' 'Danvers Half Long,' 'Imperator,' 'Gold Pak' are 7 to 9 inches long and at their streamlined best when grown in deeply dug light soil.

For heavy soils, for storage in the soil, or for freezing, the favorite with gardeners is the 'Red Cored Chantenay' and its strains—Burpee 'Goldenheart' and 'Royal Chantenay.' This is a stump-rooted, broad-shouldered type 5 to 5½ inches long.

Group the root crops — carrots, salsify, parsnips, in specially prepared soil. Raised bed plantings avoid many hazards.

"We stick with the 'Red Cored Chantenay.' Plant about 35 feet of row about July 20. Second thinnings are large enough to eat by early November and the rest grow slowly all winter and are still good eating into April, although at about that time they begin to get hairy and split. But, we have eaten them up by then." (JB)

Cauliflower

Will not head up properly in hot weather. Best grown as a fall crop.
- *Days to germination: 4 to 10*
- *Weeks to transplant size: 5 to 7*
- *Days from seed to harvest: 70 to 120*
- *Days from transplant to harvest: 55 to 65*
- *Plantings per person: 15 to 20 feet*
- *Plants per 100 feet of row: 50 to 75*
- *Yield per 100 feet of row: 50 head*

Set out transplants. When the heads begin to show through the leaves, it's time to tie the leaves together to blanch them. With the variety 'Self Blanch,' the leaves curl over the head when grown in cool weather.

If too many mature at the same time, lift plants and hang them with head downwards in a cool, airy place. Spray with water to keep fresh.

Celeriac

Celeriac or turnip-rooted celery has been developed for the root instead of the top. Its culture is the same as that of celery, and the enlarged roots can be used at any time after they are big enough (USDA).

Root enlarges just at or above the surface of the soil.
Dig when 3 or 4 inches in diameter.
- *Days to germination: 9 to 21 (use clear plastic to start)*
- *Weeks to transplant size: 10 to 12*
- *Days from transplant to harvest: 90 to 120*

Rich, light, well drained soil is especially important for celeriac. Give them the same treatment as carrots, salsify, and parsnips.

Roots will be ready to lift about mid-October and they are always better when used fresh from the ground. Unless the garden is adversely situated as to climate, cover the roots with bracken or straw and lift as required. In colder parts of the country lift in November and store the roots (after removing the foliage) in boxes of sand or peat in a frost-free room. Trim off the roots before using.

Celery

Because of the long time it takes to grow from seed to transplant size, it is best to buy transplants.
- *Days from transplant to harvest: 90 to 120*
- *Planting per person: 15 to 20 feet*
- *Plants per 100 feet of row: 200 to 300*
- *Yield per 100 feet of row: 150 to 175 stalks*

Those who like their celery green (without blanching) grow 'Summer Pascal' or 'Burpee Foodhook.'

For winter storage, grow 'Green Light' or 'Utah 52-70.'

Heavy feeder. Needs constant water supply. Late celery may be kept for early winter use by banking with earth and covering the tops with leaves or straw to keep them from freezing, or it may be dug and stored in a cellar or a cold frame with the roots well embedded in moist soil. While in storage, it must be kept as cool as possible without freezing.

Chard, Swiss

A beet developed for its tops rather than its roots. Most foolproof of all vegetables. Crop after crop of the outer leaves may be harvested without injuring the plant. Only one planting is necessary.

Chard stands hot weather and is a continuous producer of summer greens.
- *Days to germination: 7 to 10*
- *Days from seed to harvest: 55 to 65*
- *Planting per person: 10 feet*
- *Plants per 100 feet of row: 2 ounces of seed*
- *Yield per 100 feet of row: 50 to 80 pounds*

For dark green leaves and white stalks the variety is 'Fordhook Giant.' For crimson stalks the variety is 'Rhubarb Chard.' The red chard is sweeter and more tender than the regular chard.

When required, always pull the stem as for rhubarb, for cutting them will cause the roots to bleed and will reduce the crop.

"We don't need Swiss Chard in mid-summer what with all the other goodies of nature's bounty, but it's good to have in early spring before the other vegetables come along. We plant seeds around August 1. There's not a lot of production for us in the fall in our climate, but the plants get their root growth and explode as soon as weather permits in the spring." (JB)

Corn

Don't crowd the plants. Thin to 10 to 14 inches between the plants. Plant early, mid-season, and late varieties or successive plantings every 2 to 3 weeks.

- *Days to germination: 6 to 10*
- *Days from seed to harvest: 60 to 90*
- *Planting per person: 15 to 25 feet*
- *Plants per 100 feet of row: 4 ounces of seed*
- *Yield per 100 feet or row: 100 ears*

Many varieties, early and late, for example: 'Early Sunglow' (63 days), 'Jubilee' (84 days), 'Golden Cross Bantam' (85 days), 'Silver Queen' (96 days).

Check the office of your County Extension Agent for local adaptation.

In cool summer and short-season areas, choose early maturing varieties.

Corn is wind pollinated. Plant in short blocks of 3 to 4 rows, rather than a single row.

Cucumbers

The growing of cucumbers should be approached from several angles. If quantities of pickles are on the agenda, it's wise to consider the pickling varieties along with the salad or slicing varieties. If garden space is limited, cucumbers can be trained on trellises. Cucumbers that are curved when grown on the ground, grow almost straight when trained on a trellis.

In areas with summer rains the good gardener chooses varieties resistant to the diseases that plague cucumbers. Some varieties that are resistant to mosaic and mildew are: 'Early Surecrop' (58 days), 'Triumph' (63 days), 'Victory' (60 days).

- *Days to germination: 6 to 10*
- *Weeks to transplant size: 3 to 4*
- *Days from seed to harvest: 55 to 65*
- *Planting per person: 5 to 10 feet (slicing varieties)*
- *Plants per 100 feet of row: ½ ounce of seed*
- *Yield per 100 feet of row: 50 to 100 pounds or*
                              12 to 15 fruit per plant

The pickling varieties show their disease resistance in their name. The initials SMR standing for scab, mosaic, resistant.

'Wisconsin SMR 18' is one of the leading commercial and home garden varieties.

'Patio Pik' and 'Salty' are bush type, gynoecious hybrids (all female blossoms) which produce fruits close to the base of the plant.

Keep all fruits picked as they reach usable size. Even one fruit left to mature on the vine will stop the set of new fruits.

If plant is under stress from lack of moisture, it just stops growing and picks up again when moisture is applied.

Kale

No other plant is so well adapted to fall sowing throughout a wide area of both North and South or in areas characterized by winters of moderate severity. Kale may well follow some early-season vegetable such as green beans, potatoes or peas. (USDA)

- *Days to germination: 3 to 10*
- *Weeks to transplant size: 4 to 6*
- *Days from seed to harvest: 55 to 65*
- *Planting per person: 5 to 10 feet*
- *Plants per 100 feet of row: ½ ounce of seed*
- *Yield per 100 feet of row: 50 pounds*

Kohlrabi

This is a plant which is never troubled by hot, dry conditions and when the turnip is often fibrous and unpleasant, the kohlrabi retains its delicate and agreeable flavor.

- *Days to germination: 3 to 10*
- *Weeks to transplant size: 4 to 6*
- *Days from seed to harvest: 60 to 70*
- *Planting per person: 5 to 10 feet*
- *Plants per 100 feet of row: ½ ounce of seed*
- *Yield per 100 feet of row: 50 to 100 pounds*

Of the varieties 'Early White Vienna' (55 days), and 'Early Purple Vienna' (60 days), the 'Early Purple Vienna' stands better over winter.

Sowings may be made once each month from April until early July so that the early "globes" can be used when small, while those from later sowings may be left to stand over winter.

Leeks

Leeks do not bulb as onions do. The thickened stems are blanched by hilling soil around them. Plant in trenches 4 to 6 inches deep and hill soil against the stems after the plants are fairly well grown.

- *Days to germination: 7 to 12*
- *Weeks to transplant size: 10 to 12*
- *Days from seed to harvest: 140*
- *Days from transplant to harvest: 80 to 90*

Under favorable conditions, they grow to 1½ inches or more in diameter.

The plants will continue to grow until mid-November when the first liftings are made with a fork and the soil is washed away. Further liftings will take place during winter when required, for no matter how severe the weather, the plant will suffer no harm.

Where the ground does not freeze the leeks can remain in the ground through the winter and be dug when needed, or they may be stored in sand.

In cold winter areas, cover with a light straw mulch with a piece of black plastic over the top.

Lettuce

When you consider stretching the season, lettuce comes into more than ordinary attention. Lettuce production early in the season and in the fall is no problem. It's a cool weather crop that has the bad habit of bolting to seed in the longer days and warmer nights of summer. However, it's a plant that does well in partial shade, and if you choose varieties to fit the season, you can enjoy lettuce throughout a long growing season.

Know the types. Leaf lettuce. The easiest to grow. If summer heat is a problem, choose 'Salad Bowl,' 'Slobolt,' or 'Oakleaf.'

'Butterhead,' 'Summer Bibb,' and 'Buttercrunch' are the best choices where you are trying for summer harvests.

Of the crisphead varieties, 'Great Lakes' is the popular spring and fall variety. It may be bitter in hot weather. It stands up well in fall plantings. 'Ithaca' is a non-bolting, tipburn resistant variety.

- *Days to germination: 4 to 10*
- *Weeks to transplant size: 3 to 5*
- *Days from seed to harvest: Head (75-90), Leaf (45-60), Butterhead (75-80)*
- *Planting per person: 6 to 12 feet of row*
- *Yield per 100 feet of row: 100 to 200 plants*

You can save time in early spring by buying transplants. Grow in peat pots or transplant thinnings. Successive harvests of a few plants avoid lettuce glut.

Leaf lettuce, requiring such a short time from transplant to harvest, can be tucked into corners, in flower-borders, or inter-cropped between slower growing vegetables. Lettuce is a great crop to play with. You can, by choice of varieties, get leaf color and texture to liven up the salad bowl. You can lengthen the harvest season dramatically by the use of a lettuce box or cold frame that will protect the earliest and latest plantings and, by shading, allow summer harvests.

Bird protection is necessary with all varieties as seeds germinate. The birds show their variety preference as lettuce becomes older. Our birds work on 'Ruby,' even in the transplant size.

Every day must be a growing day with lettuce. If growth is checked by lack of nutrients or moisture, the plant never fully recovers. Wise gardeners fertilize the soil before planting.

Give lettuce room to grow. Head lettuce should be thinned to 12 to 14 inches between plants. Head lettuce can be enjoyed in the early stages of growth, when the leaves are loosely folded. But, it needs room to grow.

While it's true that leaf lettuce can be harvested a leaf at a time and thinning is not as important as with head lettuce, you miss out on the tender light green leaves in the center of the almost mature plant. Don't crowd the plants. A vigorous variety such as 'Salad Bowl' should be spaced 10 inches apart.

Onion

The onion grows tops in cool weather and forms bulbs in warm weather. However, the timing of bulbing is controlled by both temperature and day length. Varieties are classed by long-day and short-day. Most varieties grown in the North require 14 to 16 hours of daylight. In the South, onions grow through the cool fall and winter and bulb at about 12 hours when the weather warms in spring. In order to get fall growth of tops before the long-day bulbing time in the North, seedlings are grown in the South and shipped North for early-set transplants.

The growing of onions and its forms and relatives for year around use is a challenge every gardener must meet. How do you handle your soil and planting times for green onions, Egyptian onions, dry onions, leeks, shallots, chives and garlic? The 12-monther will find the answers by reading and good old trial-and-error.

We are concerned, on these pages, with extending the growing season with onions for storage.

The best storage varieties are the late maturing *pungent* onions. Those with short, shriveled necks. Examples: 'Southport White Globe,' 'Southport Red Globe,' 'Red Granex,' 'Early Yellow Globe,' 'Ebenezer,' and 'Autumn Spice.'

Parsley (Rooted)

For winter storage, the variety of parsley is the 'Hamburg' or 'Turnip Rooted.' It forms a slender root 8 to 10 inches long.
- *Days to germination: 14 to 28*
- *Weeks to transplant size: 8*
- *Days from seed to harvest: 85 to 90*
- *Planting per person: 10 to 15 feet*
- *Plants per 100 feet of row: ½ ounce of seed*
- *Yield per 100 feet of row: 50 pounds*

Has parsley-like flavor when used raw or grated in salads, but a flavor more like celeriac when cooked.

May be stored in the ground but is best lifted and stored in sand.

Parsnips

Winter cold is a must for this root vegetable. Cold, near the freezing point, changes starch to sugar and gives the parsnip the sweet, nut-like flavor for which it is famous.

Parsnip roots may be left in the ground all winter or dug in the late fall and stored in moist sand. In warm winter areas the roots continue growth and become tough and woody.
- *Days to germination: 15 to 25*
- *Days from seed to harvest: 100 to 120*
- *Planting per person: 10 to 15 feet*
- *Plants per 100 feet of row: ½ ounce of seed*
- *Yield per 100 feet of row: 100 pounds*

Roots develop to a length of 12 to 18 inches and become distorted in a heavy, rough soil.

Give parsnips, carrots and salsify a special deeply dug soil to which generous amounts of organic matter have been added.

If water table is high or the soil becomes waterlogged, a raised bed, all above ground, will protect roots from rot, and make digging a lot easier.

Peas

Definitely a cool weather crop. Hardy enough to be planted as soon as the ground can be worked in the spring in cold winter areas, and in the fall where winters are mild.
- *Days to germination: 6 to 15*
- *Days from seed to harvest: 65 to 85*
- *Planting per person: 10 to 15 feet*
- *Plants per 100 feet of row: 1 pound of seed*
- *Yield per 100 feet of row: 50 to 75 pounds*

See page 9 for variations in days from seed to harvest by varieties, and time of planting.

The Edible-Podded Sugar Peas (Snow Peas) can be planted in September for a winter crop in mild winter areas.

The higher the temperature, the more quickly they pass the edible stage.

"We plant a few peas in late October which get a head start of a few days on peas we plant in early spring, i.e. mid-February. Those few days seem important when you're hungry for fresh peas." (JB)

Peppers

A warm-weather crop. Don't set transplants out until weather has warmed. When night time temperatures are below 55°, the small plants just sit, turn yellow and become stunted. Plants never fully recover.

Like tomato plants, pepper will fail to set fruit at low night temperatures.

Expect some blossom drop when daytime temperatures climb above 90° but fruit setting will resume when weather moderates. Small fruited varieties are more tolerant to high temperatures.
- *Days to germination: 10 to 20*
- *Weeks to transplant size: 6 to 8*
- *Days from transplant to harvest: 60 to 80*
- *Planting per person: 5 feet or 2 to 3 plants*
- *Plants per 100 feet of row: ½ ounce of seed*
- *Yield per 100 feet of row: 400 fruit or 40 pounds*

Cut off mature fruit to keep plant producing. Use pruning shears or sharp knife. Leave ½-inch of stem on the peppers for better storage.

"Since peppers have such a short harvest season, and so many are ready at once, we suggest that the largest harvests be stuffed, precooked, popped into freezer for winter consumption." (SH)

Potatoes

Potatoes, when grown under favorable conditions, are one of the most productive of all vegetables, in terms of food per unit area of land.

Potatoes (tubers) do not grow on the roots. They form *above* the seed piece on underground stems. The usual planting method is to set seed pieces 4" deep and when plants are 5 to 6 inches high, to hill up the plants with soil from between the rows. This is necessary because many of the tubers form at ground level.

Potatoes exposed to light, either in garden or storage, turn green and become inedible.
- *Days from planting tubers to harvest: 90 to 105*
- *Planting per person: 50 to 100 feet*

- *Plants per 100 feet of row: 5 to 8 pounds of tubers*
- *Yield per 100 feet of row: 60 to 100 pounds*

You can start potatoes with storebought potatoes. However, they may carry diseases and some may have been treated to prevent sprouting. Best to buy certified seed potatoes.

Freshly dug potatoes won't sprout until they have had a rest period.

You can harvest small new potatoes as soon as the plant blooms. They will reach full size when the tops die down.

One potato vine will yield from 6 to 9 pounds of potatoes.

Store in a dark, frost-free, screened place.

You can *pick* potatoes rather than *dig* them by hilling over the potatoes with peat moss, sawdust or straw.

"New" potatoes may be enjoyed all year round if a quantity are placed in a metal biscuit tin filled with dry peat and buried 12 inches deep in the garden, a stone marking the position.

Radish

A "catch crop" that can be tucked in most anywhere. Intercrop with lettuce, spinach or early beets.

- *Days to germination: 3 to 10*
- *Days from seed to harvest: 20 to 50*
- *Planting per person: 5 to 10 feet*
- *Plants per 100 feet of row: 1 ounce of seed*
- *Yield per 100 feet of row: 25 pounds*

Thin seedlings to 1 to 2 inches apart very soon after emergence to allow roots to expand.

Most frequent disaster is damage from cabbage maggot. Dust DIAZINON granules in planting furrow when sowing seeds.

Rhubarb

Rhubarb is started from rooted crowns (divisions). It can be grown from seed but results are variable. The root divisions offered by your local garden store are selected for quality and climate adaptability.

The varieties adapted to the northern United States and Canada require two months of temperatures around freezing to break their rest period. And for best quality and yield, they need a long cool spring. The popular varieties—'Ruby,' 'MacDonald,' 'Valentine Red'—are for cold winter areas. The most widely planted California variety is 'Giant Cherry.'

- *Seedlings variable: Buy crown division*
- *Time from transplant to harvest: Allow all stalks to grow the first year. Harvest for 1 to 2 weeks the second year. After that, harvests of 8 weeks or more are possible.*
- *Plants per person: 1 to 2 crowns.*

Give rhubarb room to grow—3 feet between plants. Locate where it won't get in the way of annual operation. Planted in deeply dug, enriched soil the plant should produce for 10 years.

In harvesting, the stalks are pulled, not cut. Only the leaf stalks are edible. Leaf blades contain a high amount of oxalic acid and are poisonous.

Rutabaga

Cool weather vegetable and hardy to cold. Hardier than turnips. Plant as late as possible for fall and winter use.

Most satisfactory in northern areas.

- *Days to germination: 5 to 10*
- *Days from seed to harvest: 80 to 90*
- *Plants per 100 feet of row: ¼ ounce of seed*
- *Yield per 100 feet of row: 150 pounds*

The variety 'Purple Top Yellow' (90 days) is a good keeper.

May be left in the ground during winter and lifted when required.

Salsify

This is the Vegetable Oyster.

As a long-root crop, it requires a deep, crumbly soil. Group with other slow-growing root crops.

- *Days to germination: 5 to 10*
- *Days from seed to harvest: 110 to 150*
- *Planting per person: 10 to 15 feet*
- *Plants per 100 feet of row: ½ ounce of seed*
- *Yield per 100 feet of row: 75 pounds*

The variety 'Sandwich Island Mammoth' (150 days) grows 8 to 9 inches long and 1¾ inches in diameter, tapering slightly from the shoulder to the end.

Salsify may be left in the ground over winter or lifted and stored like parsnips or other root crops.

Spinach

A hardy, cool-weather plant that withstands winter conditions in the South. In most of the North, spinach is primarily an early spring and late fall crop, but in some areas, where summer temperatures are mild, it may be grown continuously from early spring until late fall. (USDA)

- *Days to germination: 6 to 14*
- *Days from seed to harvest: 40 to 50*
- *Planting per person: 10 to 20 feet*
- *Plants per 100 feet of row: 1 ounce of seed*
- *Yield per 100 feet of row: 40 to 50 pounds*

For early spring planting the most popular variety is 'Long Standing Bloomsdale' (48 days).

For fall and winter harvests: 'Winter Bloomsdale' (45 days) is hardy enough to winter over from a fall planting where winters are mild.

Spinach is very sensitive to acid soils. If a soil test shows the need, apply lime to the part of the garden used for spinach, regardless of the treatment given the rest of the area.

Squash and Pumpkin

Call the squashes and pumpkins the most efficient of the vegetables. The summer squash, if handled right, generally exceeds any estimated yield. The winter squash creates its own hard-shelled winter storage protection.

For a long harvest of summer squash, keep the plant producing by picking the fruit when it's young and tender. If fruits are allowed to grow large on the plant, the yield will be much reduced. If daily yield is too much for current use, the surplus may be parboiled and frozen for use later in casseroles, breads, etc.

The winter varieties are most important to the 12-month gardener. They can be stored for a long period if allowed to fully mature. Pick them before hard frost. Cut stems from the vine. Fruit without stems does not store well. Fruits are ripe when they are hard to the fingernail.

Winter squash varieties are divided into three groups: *Acorn or Danish type*—baking squash with a mild, nut-like flavor. 'Table Ace' (76 days) semibush; 'Table King' (80 days) bush; 'Table Queen Ebony' (85 days) large vine.

Maxima type—small to large squash that are baked, steamed, boiled, or used for pie. 'Gold Nugget' (85 days) small bush; 'Buttercup' (100 days) medium-sized, large vine; 'Hubbard' (110 days) blue or green skin, large vine; 'Banana' (110 days) large fruit, large vine.

Butternut type—small squash that is baked, steamed or boiled. The variety 'Butternut' (95 days) produces on a large vine. 'Butternut' squash can be used as a substitute for sweet potatoes and pie pumpkins. When parboiled, mashed and seasoned with salt, pepper, and butter it rates equal to mashed sweet potatoes. We use this squash for pies in preference to pie pumpkins.

"This fall we put in our cellar a dozen banana squash, one of them 32" long, which will keep until January; about 40 'Butternut' squash, which will keep somewhat longer; 11 'Blue Hubbard,' three of which weighed over 50#, and which should keep until March or April; about 50 'Buttercups,' which resemble 'Hubbard' in taste. We are enjoying 3 distinct flavors and several variations in preparation." (JB) One of the squash recipes at the Bridgman's is "Butternut Squash Soup." You'll give it and this squash high marks when you try it. Here's the recipe:

Butternut Squash Soup

4 cups chicken bouillon (from cubes)
3 medium onions, peeled and halved
3 cups butternut squash, peeled, seeded and cut up
5 whole cloves
½ pint heavy cream or non-dairy substitute
1 teaspoon curry powder
chopped parsley (optional)

Cook onions, squash, and cloves in the bouillon until just soft. Pour entire mixture into a blender. Add curry powder and heavy cream and blend 2 to 3 minutes. Serve sprinkled with chopped parsley. Also good with hot dogs.

For producing pounds of food per square foot of soil, the squash and pumpkin rate high. The following yields were recorded from a planting on black plastic mulch at the Illinois Experiment Station at Simpson, Illinois:

4 plants of zucchini produced 52 pounds
7 plants of bush 'Table King' produced 39 pounds
13 plants of bush pumpkin 'Cinderella' produced 306 pounds.

PUMPKIN. Some are grown for pies, some for jack-o-lanterns, some for competition in size, and some for their seeds. Just as there are new bush-type winter squash, there are bush pumpkins. 'Cinderella' (95 days) produces 10-inch Halloween pumpkins on a 5-foot wide bush. 'Small Sugar' (100 days) is a large jack-o-lantern type. 'Big Max' (120 days) is not a table variety but a contest winner for size. 'Lady Godiva' (100 days) is grown for its "naked" or hulless seeds. Squash, pumpkin and sweet potatoes require special storage conditions — temperatures at 55° with good, *dry* air circulation.

Sweet Potatoes

Sweet potatoes may be grown wherever there is a frost-free period of about 150 days with relatively high temperatures. Plants (slips) are produced from roots (in hot beds) covered with 2 inches of sand or planter mix.

Best to buy plants at your garden store. Slips are set in open ground after soil is warm.

• *Days from transplant to harvest: 120*
• *Planting per person: 20 to 40 feet*
• *Plants per 100 feet of row: 100*
• *Yield per 100 feet of row: 80 to 100 pounds*

Varieties most frequently recommended: Dry fleshed: 'Nemagold' and 'Nugget'; moist fleshed: 'Porto Rico,' 'Gold Rush,' 'Centennial.'

Dig potatoes before frost. In using a spading fork, take care not to bruise or injure the roots. Let the roots take the sun for 2 or 3 hours to dry thoroughly; then put them in containers and place in a warm room to cure. The proper curing temperature is 85°F. Curing for about 10 days is followed by storage at 50° to 55°. (USDA)

Tomatoes

We assume that by now every gardener has become an expert tomato grower. For a complete guide, we recommend ORTHO's book, *All About Vegetables*.

The 12-monthers remind us:

1. In rainy fall weather, plastic covering of the vines will prolong the harvest. See photo.
2. The green tomato has many uses.
3. Harvest of ripe tomatoes can be extended for weeks by hanging vines in a frost-free garage or shed. Tomatoes that show signs of ripening in the garden will continue to ripen on the pulled vines.
4. If you like the pickled cocktail size tomato, plant the variety 'Small Fry.'
5. The tomato grower who has had "bad luck" due to disease, should choose varieties of known disease resistance. In seed catalogs and on tags at the nursery look for the letters that signify their resistance: "V" for verticillium wilt, "F" for fusarium wilt, and "N" for nematodes. Here are some well known examples: 'Small Fry' VF (52 days), 'Early Girl' V (54 days), 'Spring Giant' VF (68 days), 'Heinz 1350' VF (75 days), 'Better Boy' VFN (72 days), 'Jet Star' VF (72 days), 'Tropic' VF (82 days), 'Manalucie' F (86 days).

Both verticillium and fusarium live over in the soil. Avoid growing tomatoes in the same soil year after year. Some gardeners avoid disease trouble by growing tomatoes in plastic garbage cans filled with one of the disease-free soil mixes.

Turnip

A cool-season crop. Best for early spring or fall crops.

Easy to grow. Quick to mature.

• *Days to germination: 3 to 10*
• *Days from seed to harvest: 45 to 60*
• *Planting per person per year: 30 feet*
• *Plants per 100 feet of row: ½ ounce of seed*
• *Yield per 100 feet of row: 100 to 150 pounds of roots*
        50 pounds of greens

Harvest early varieties, such as 'Tokyo Cross' (35 days) before they get pithy — usually 2 inches in diameter. Sow 'Purple Top White Globe' (60 days) for fall and winter use.

Roots of 'Purple Top' are crisp when 4 inches across. Will store in the soil for winter use. Turnips and rutabagas not only store well in the ground, but when stored in the basement they give off odors.

Storage temperatures. To give each vegetable the optimum temperature, humidity and air circulation needed for long storage life is not easy without building temperature controlled storage rooms. The casual 12-monther tries to approximate his basement, pit or garage to these conditions. (They are far easier to create in cold winter areas than where winters are mild.)

For the following crops, low temperature (32°-40°) and high humidities are best: beets, carrots, celeriac, celery, kohlrabi, parsnips, rutabagas, salsify and turnips.

Onions and garlic: Low temperature (32°), dry air and good air circulation.

Green tomatoes: Warm temperature (55°-70°), little air circulation.

Canning

and other related methods of preserving the fruit and vegetable harvest.

◁

Back then, you had to keep the fires stoked in the cookstove, if you were going to keep ahead of the harvest. Here a picking of apples was made into apple sauce and an apple pie.

The different methods of preserving the harvest each have special points in their favor. While everyone has an opinion, I think that certain fruits and vegetables taste better when canned than when preserved by any other method.

The canning procedure may appear difficult at first, but like anything else, once you get the hang of it, you'll wonder why you didn't try it long before. If you've never done any canning, it's sometimes easier to share the first experience with a friend, neighbor, or relative. Not only can you share in the original expense of the canning equipment and produce, but an extra pair of hands can be a great help the first couple of times you run through the procedure.

The two basic methods of canning are explained in detail on the next two pages. Many of the recipes which follow in the chapter will refer back to one of these methods. There is a reason for each step, so be sure to follow the instructions carefully.

How you can, generally depends on *what* food is being canned, the canning material, and the length of storage desired. Vegetables, meats, fish, and poultry are low in acid and can be safely processed *only* in a steam pressure canner which supplies enough sustained heat (240° F) to kill botulism bacteria. The small pressure cooker saucepan designed for fast cooking should *not* be used for canning.

Most fruits and some acid vegetables can be canned with the boiling water bath method which supplies enough heat, without overcooking, to destroy organisms that might cause spoilage.

The other method is the boiling water bath, used for most fruits and some acid vegetables. The boiling water bath supplies enough heat to destroy organisms which might cause spoilage, without overcooking the food inside the jars.

As always there are some exceptions to every rule. You can increase the acid content in some food and thus make it safe for boiling water bath canning, by adding considerable amounts of lemon juice or vinegar. Keep in mind, though, the one rule to follow when canning at home: "Always follow the rules." I will only discuss recipes that have been tested and used with success. And I repeat, don't take any shortcuts or experiment when canning. Follow exactly the times and temperatures listed in the instructions, and start with good quality produce for a good quality product.

Canning cherries by boiling water bath

Start with 2½ pounds of cherries per finished quart. Figure out how many jars your canner will hold. Mine holds 7 quarts so I use 17-18 pounds of cherries. Wash and sort the cherries. Stem and pit them or prick each one you intend to leave unpitted with a sterilized darning needle. This prevents the skin from bursting during canning. If pressed for time, leave the pits, and remember not to serve that batch to small children. The pits add flavor, but be sure to warn any of the small children who will be eating the canned fruit.

In a 7 quart kettle dissolve 2 cups sugar in 2 cups warm water. When the syrup is clear, add the cherries. Add 6 or 7 inches of water to the canning kettle and place on a low burner. Keep the water medium hot, but don't boil. Make sure the rack is in place.

When you have enough cherries in the syrup to fill about 1 jar, bring the mixture to a boil. Pack one of the jars using a funnel so the juice and pulp won't get on the lip of the jar.

When the jar is filled to the shoulder remove the funnel, re-check the lip, secure the lid, and seal with the ring. Make sure it's secure, but not overly tight. The lid has to have some freedom to expand in the canning process. Add the jars to the kettle.

As the syrup heats continue to add cherries. Bring them to a boil and jar until all 7 are full. You'll pick up the rhythm soon and the jars will seem to fill like magic.

As you work on jar number 7, turn the kettle burner on high and let it come to a boil. When you add the last jar, be sure the water covers the jars by at least two inches.

When the canner comes to a boil, reduce the heat so the water will bubble slightly. Some of the liquid will boil out if you cook too fast, you'll end up with half-filled jars and wasted syrup.

After 15 minutes remove the canner from the heat and take each jar from the kettle with tongs. Place on a folded towel and cover all seven with another towel to keep cooling air from the boiling jars. In just a few minutes you hear a pleasant "ring" as the lids seal.

If some fail to seal (and don't worry, it happens), place in the refrigerator and use for meals. You'll often find that the unsealed jars had an imperfection on the lip. Perhaps you failed to use a funnel and pulp accumulated on the lip. Sometimes the lid was not quite tight enough.

Heat processing canned food

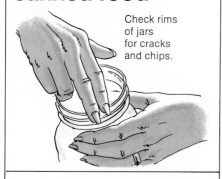

Check rims of jars for cracks and chips.

Sterilize jars, caps, and lids.

Leave recommended head space when filling jars

Head space

Remove bubbles with a knife or narrow spatula

There are two basic methods of heat processing canned foods. The first is the "boiling water bath" (sometimes called "simmering water bath"). The boiling water bath method is used for foods naturally *high in acid*. Examples of high acid foods are, all fresh fruits, fruit juices, and fruit purées. Cucumber pickles and tomatoes can also be safely canned using the boiling water bath method, but make sure the tomatoes are not one of the new "low-acid" varieties.

The other process is "steam pressure canning"; this method is *always* used for all *low-acid* foods such as, vegetables, meats, poultry, and fish. Inside the pressure canner, the combination of steam and pressure raises the temperature of the food inside the jars to 240 degrees. It is only when low acid foods are processed at this temperature, for the length of time designated in the recipe, that botulism bacteria are destroyed. *Always process low-acid foods using the steam pressure canner method.*

Boiling water bath

Large kettles, made especially for canning, can be purchased commercially. They are sometimes referred to as "cold pack canners." Water bath canners can also be made

at home, using any large kettle or pail, one which is deep enough to permit water to cover the jars at least 2-inches over the tops, with a little extra space to allow for the boiling.

You'll also need a rack that fits in the bottom of the kettle (the commercial set-ups come equipped) to hold the jars at least ½-inch above the bottom of the canner. You can use an old refrigerator rack, or construct one from strips of wood or wire, just as long as the rack allows the boiling water to circulate under the jars.

The canner should also have a proper-fitting lid which makes it easier to maintain the proper temperature during the processing.

Assemble all the equipment needed before you start: the pressure canner for low-acid foods, the boiling-water kettle for high-acid foods, jars and caps, jar lifter, funnel, measuring utensils, timer, and the recipe and instructions.

1) Examine the tops of the jars, making sure there are no nicks, cracks, or sharp edges that would prevent a good seal. Any imperfect jars should not be used for canning.

2) Wash the jars thoroughly in hot,

soapy water. Rinse completely. Keep the jars in hot water until you are ready to fill them.

Place the lids to the jars in a pan and pour boiling water over them. Do not boil but make sure the water stays hot until you are ready to use them.

Put the rack in the canning kettle and fill the kettle half full with hot water. Cover the kettle with the lid and place on the range. Heat the water, but do not boil. Keep a tea kettle full of hot water, which will be needed later, when all the jars are filled and sealed.

3) Prepare the food to be packed into the jars according to recipe directions. Fill the jars; a canning funnel makes this a less messy job. Leave the amount of head space indicated in the recipe.

4) Using a spatula, remove any air bubbles in the jar.

Wipe the rim of the jar with a clean, damp cloth. Bits of food left on the rim can prevent a jar from sealing.

5) Place prepared lid on jar; the side with the sealing compound next to the glass. Screw ring band on firmly tight. Use full strength of the hand.

6) After each jar is filled and sealed place it in the canning kettle. When

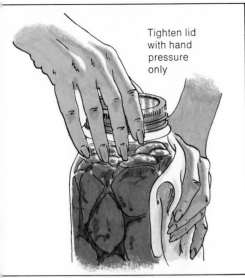

Tighten lid with hand pressure only

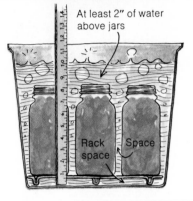

At least 2″ of water above jars

Rack space   Space

Always lift jars straight up from water with a jar lifter—don't tip them

Pressure gauge

Steam valve and petcock

Pressure regulator

Press the center of the lid to test the seal

the canning kettle has been filled with the jars, pour hot water from the teakettle, covering the jars at least 2-inches. Cover the canner and bring the water to a boil. Once the water boils, begin counting the processing time, keeping the water at a hard simmer the entire time.

7) After processing for the proper time, lift jars from kettle using a jar lifter.

8) Set processed jars 2 or 3 inches apart on several thicknesses of cloth or on a rack to cool. Do not set hot jars in a draft or on a cold, wet surface, and do not cover.

9) After the jars are cool the screw band can be removed. Test the lid for a good seal by pressing the lid with your finger—if the lid is curved down and will not move, the jar is sealed.

Steam pressure canning

A steam pressure canner is a heavy kettle, large enough to accommodate canning jars, with a locking lid which forms a steam-tight seal. The lid of the kettle contains a safety valve, a petcock and a pressure gauge. Don't let all the equipment scare you—steam pressure canners are simple to use once you're familiar with the process.

There are two different types of

pressure canners available; one has a weighted gauge which automatically limits the pressure to a pre-set level; the other type has a dial gauge which registers the amount of pressure inside the canner.

Before each canning season, be sure to check the gasket. If you have the dial gauge type canner, check the gauge to make sure it reads accurately.

To steam pressure can, set the rack in the bottom of the canner and fill with 2-3 inches of boiling water. Place on the range and keep the water hot.

At this point follow the instructions given for the boiling water bath, through step number 5, preparing the food according to the individual recipe.

As each jar is filled and sealed, place in the canner to keep the food hot. Space the jars so they do not touch each other or the sides of the canner.

Fasten the lid of the canner securely, leaving the petcock open, or the vent pipe uncovered, depending on what kind of canner you have.

The pressure canner must be vented, or exhausted before you actually start processing. The term

"vent" means to let steam escape from the petcock or vent for at least 10 minutes.

After the canner has been vented, close the petcock, or put the weighted gauge on, and bring the canner to the proper pressure by adjusting the heat of the stove. During the processing time make sure the pressure never falls below the required level. Start counting the processing time as soon as the proper pressure level has been reached.

After the jars have been processed for the required time remove the canner from the heat. Don't make any attempt to lower the pressure—let the canner sit until the hand on the pressure gauge returns to zero (about 2-3 minutes). For canners with weight gauges, nudge the weight slightly. If no steam escapes the pressure has returned to zero. Remove the weighted gauge, or slowly remove the petcock. Allow the canner to cool for approximately 15 minutes.

Remove the lid, opening it away from your face to avoid the steam, and let the jars cool in the canner for another 10 to 15 minutes; do not disturb the jars during this period.

At this point follow directions 7 and 9 given for the boiling water bath.

27

Canning jars have had a long history but the principal has remained the same. Some of the jars in this picture date back to the early 1900's, too precious for everyday use, but good for storing dried herbs and beans.

Cold packing

Here's a variation for cherry canning. Pack cold into each jar and wait until all seven are full. Use a long spouted teakettle to pour in the boiling syrup. Seal and process like you did in the first recipe. See page 25. Since you are starting with unheated cherries, cook for 25 minutes.

This way is less messy, since you pit the cherries and drop them right into the jars, avoiding the heating kettle. You can also pack the cherries more compactly, using the cold-pack method.

Homemade canned pie filling

Beginning California 4-H members make this recipe in food preservation classes. Use 10 pounds of fruit such as apricots, peaches, or apples. Wash, sort, and peel if necessary. Core and pit and cut fruit into equal-sized slices. In a small bowl combine 1 cup plus 2 tablespoons quick-cooking tapioca, 1½ cups sugar, and ¾ cup lemon juice; reserve.

Place prepared fruit in a kettle with 4 cups sugar and just enough water to keep mixture from burning. Stirring, heat to 190 degrees F. Add reserved lemon juice mixture and, stirring, reheat to 190 degrees. Using a funnel, pack into hot sterilized jars, wipe lip of jars if necessary, and seal. Process by boiling-water-bath method (see page 26) for 5 minutes. Work quickly but carefully. The 5-minute processing time goes fast, so have

the tongs and folded towel ready. Don't forget to make accurate labels for your pie filling. The fruit goes nicely, right from the jar, in little tart shells, decorated with whipped cream.

Apple-raisin pie filling

Similar to a popular commercial product, this raisin-apple filling is easy to make at home. Place 1 pound raisins and 2 cups water in a kettle. Bring to a boil, then remove from heat, cover, and set aside for 2 hours. Peel, core, and slice 1 pound cooking apples. Add to the steeped raisins along with ¾ cup sugar, 3 tablespoons corn syrup, ½ cup water, and ⅓ cup lemon juice. Heat until boiling, then simmer until apples are tender. Ladle into hot sterilized jars, seal and process by the boiling-water-bath method for 5 minutes. Keep water at a gentle boil.

Jams and jellies

Jams and jellies are a popular homemade product even with "noncanners." Jams are the easiest to make since you make them from crushed fruit or purée. Depending on the fruit used, pectin and acid may or may not be added.

Clear jellies, made from the juice of fruits or berries, must contain pectin, sugar, and acid in a definite relationship to all of the other ingredients. Some fruits such as tart apples, currants, and quince have enough natural pectin and acid to jell. With

others, such as guavas, raspberries, and apricots, you may need to add pectin or acid or both. Jam and jelly recipes packed with commercially prepared liquid and powdered pectin are excellent. I always save the recipe folders in case one of my favorite recipes is not reprinted the following year.

Homemade pectin

Homemade pectin is easy and fun to make if you have access to a supply of small early apples. In our area, June apples are the best—they are a tart hard-ripe apple. Use a mixture of ripe and slightly under-ripe apples.

Wash, quarter, core, and thinly slice the unpeeled apples into a kettle. For each pound of fruit add 2 cups water.

Cover and boil slowly for 15 minutes. Strain through a colander lined with cheesecloth and reserve the juice.

Return the apple pulp to the kettle and add the same amount of water that you originally used. Cook again for 15 minutes, let stand for 10 minutes, then re-strain through cheesecloth. Squeeze well to extract all the juice.

Combine the two batches of juice. If you began with 1 pound of apples you should have 1 quart of liquid pectin. Refrigerate until ready to use. For longer storage, heat to a boil, pour into hot sterilized jars, and seal.

To use homemade pectin. This recipe is for a very simple jam or jelly. Mix

2 cups homemade pectin with 2 cups fruit pulp and 2 cups sugar. Boil slowly until the mixture reaches 221 degrees, the jelling point at sea level.

Pectin test. If you are not sure whether the fruit you are working with contains enough natural pectin, try this pectin test. Add 1 teaspoon of any cooked purée or pure juice to 1 tablespoon rubbing alcohol.

Do not taste, but watch the action between the fruit and the alcohol. If the fruit is rich in pectin it will form a jellied mass stiff enough to pick up with a fork. If low in pectin, it will form small flaky pieces that cannot be picked up.

For further testing, add 1 tablespoon liquid pectin to 1 cup of cooked fruit purée or juice. Remove 1 teaspoon, combine with 1 tablespoon rubbing alcohol, and test again. If it still doesn't jell, add 1 more tablespoon liquid pectin to the cup of fruit. Remove another teaspoon and test with another tablespoon of alcohol. *Be sure to discard the samples tested.* The alcohol contains a poison. Once you determine how many tablespoons of pectin you'll need per cup of fruit, just multiply that by the number of total cups of fruit used. For instance, if you had to add 3 tablespoons pectin to your cup of fruit before it would jell in your sampling, then you'll need 9 tablespoons liquid pectin for 3 cups of fruit.

Converting powdered pectin to liquid pectin

When you cannot find liquid pectin it is useful to know how to turn the powdered form into liquid. Mix 1 package powdered pectin in ½ cup water and boil for 1 minute. Pour into a measuring cup and add enough water to make 1 cup. Use as you would liquid pectin.

Acid testing

Remember, the best jams and jellies need acid as well as pectin. Compare, by taste, the tartness of the fruit you are using with a mixture of 1 teaspoon lemon juice, 3 tablespoons water, and ½ cup sugar. If the fruit is not as tart as the mixture then add 1 tablespoon lemon juice to the entire batch of fruit. Taste again, and again compare the tartness with the lemon mixture. If the fruit is very ripe and extra sweet, you may have to add extra lemon.

Test for jelling point

A cooking thermometer is a good investment and makes your recipes nearly foolproof when you know the jelling point. The jelling point is 221 degrees F. at sea level.
To test at your elevation, boil water to see at what temperature it boils, then add 9 degrees F. for the jelling point.

The sheet test can also be used to check the jelling point. Dip a spoon into the boiling syrup. Tilt the spoon until the syrup runs out. When the jelling point is reached, the last two drops will run together and flake or sheet from the spoon.

To get a good jell, be sure to follow the recipe accurately. Cook in small batches and do not double a recipe.

Sealing jams and jellies

Many people still use paraffin for sealing jams and jellies but I find that during summer with hot days and cool nights, it expands and contracts. The jelly may seep up around the paraffin and mold. Peaches, pears, and apricots are particularly susceptible. The product is safe if you remove the mold, but it looks unappetizing.

The most reliable method of sealing preserves is to put them in regular canning jars with lids that seal. Use hot sterilized jars, lids, and screw bands. As soon as you fill each jar, wipe the rim with a clean damp cloth. Place lid on jar and screw on ring band as tightly as you comfortably can. Let cool, then press lid with your finger. If it stays down, it is sealed.

When I haven't been able to find canning lids or jars, I use washed and sterilized baby food jars or some of the other jars such as peanut butter jars that have a type of sealing compound that stays inside the lids. When you pour in the hot jam or jelly, the sealing compound softens and you almost always get a good seal.

The most important thing is to keep things very clean as you work, and work quickly when pouring and sealing any open kettle product. The faster you fill and seal a jar, the less chance of unfavorable bacteria working its way into the cooling jam. Seal each jar in turn. Do not wait until all the jars are filled.

Crabapple jelly

10 cups crabapples, cored and
    coarsely chopped
2 cups water
2 cups vinegar
6 cinnamon sticks
36 whole cloves

1. Place chopped apples in a kettle with water, vinegar, and cinnamon sticks and cloves tied in a little bag.

2. Mix and cook gently until soft.

3. Remove the spice bag.

4. Separate juice from fruit by pouring through a jelly bag. Hang over a pot and let the juice drip out overnight, or for at least several hours. Don't rush the process. Let it drip at its own rate. You might do this job before bedtime, so you won't be tempted to squeeze the bag. If you give in to temptation, the liquid will become cloudy. Let the juice drip out slowly by itself to get a good clear jelly. To prevent an accident tie the jelly bag to the water faucet and hang over a pot placed in the sink.

5. The next day measure the juice and for each cup of crabapple juice add ¾ cup sugar.

6. Cook to the jelling point, stirring often.

7. Pour into hot sterilized jars and seal.

Pomegranate jelly

4 cups pomegranate juice
7½ cups sugar
3 tablespoons lemon juice
1 bottle liquid pectin

To juice the pomegranates move the whole operation outside, and *remember,* pomegranates do not discriminate against what and whom they stain.

1. Cover yourself and everything you use with plastic wrap. Use an electric orange juicer to squeeze the halved pomegranates or separate and crush the edible portion with a potato masher. You'll have lots of clear juice and a terrible mess.

2. Mix pomegranate juice, sugar, and lemon juice in a large saucepan. Bring to a boil and immediately add liquid pectin; boil rapidly for exactly 30 seconds, stirring constantly.

3. Remove from heat, skim, and pour quickly into eleven 8-ounce sterilized jars and seal.

Elderberry jelly

3 pounds elderberries
1 lemon
1 package powdered pectin
4½ cups sugar

1. Clean and sort elderberries.

2. Heat over low heat, adding just enough water to keep the fruit from burning, until the juices begin to flow. Simmer slowly for 15 minutes.

3. Pour through a jelly bag and let drain overnight. Remember for clear jelly, do not squeeze the bag to extract the juice.

4. In the morning measure 3 cups of juice.

5. Add the lemon juice and pectin. Bring to a full boil.

6. Add 4½ cups sugar and boil 1 minute only, stirring constantly.

7. Remove from heat, skim off any foam, pour into hot sterilized jars, and seal.

Spiced orange slices

4 oranges
1 quart water
2 cups sugar
1¼ cups water
½ cup wine vinegar
¼ teaspoon ground ginger
12 whole cloves
3 cinnamon sticks

1. Place whole oranges in a pan with 1 quart of water and bring to a boil. Simmer gently for 30 minutes, but do not overcook or the oranges will fall apart.

2. Drain and cut in crosswise slices.

3. In a heavy kettle combine sugar, water, wine vinegar, ginger, and cloves and cinnamon sticks tied in a cheesecloth bag. Bring slowly to a boil, stirring until the sugar dissolves.

4. Add the orange slices and simmer for 20 minutes. Remove bag.

5. Spoon into hot sterilized jars and seal. Makes 6 cups.

Spiced blueberry preserves

1 quart blueberries
¼ cup cider vinegar
2 cups sugar
¼ teaspoon ground allspice
¼ teaspoon ground cinnamon
⅛ teaspoon ground cloves

1. Wash and stem blueberries.

2. Combine in a heavy pan with cider vinegar, sugar, allspice, cinnamon, and cloves.

3. Cook until thick, stirring often.

To test, place a spoonful on a refrigerated plate and see if it is thick enough for your taste. This is the consistency the preserves will have when cold. Or, use a spoon to make the sheet test (see page 29). If it has not reached the jelling point, cook a little longer.

4. Pack into hot sterilized jars and seal.

Pickled Pears

4 dozen small pears, firm and ripe
1 tablespoon mixed pickling spice
1 teaspoon whole cloves
1 piece ginger root, optional
1 lemon thinly sliced
1 cup brown sugar
2 cups sugar
2½ cups water
1½ cups white vinegar

1. Peel pears, leave stems intact. If pears are large, cut into quarters.

2. Tie pickling spices, cloves, and ginger root in a small cheesecloth bag.

3. Put all of the ingredients except the pears in a kettle and bring to a boil. Reduce heat and simmer for five minutes.

4. Add the pears to the syrup, a layer at a time, and cook gently until tender, about 15 minutes.

5. Carefully remove pears from syrup and set aside. Repeat layering of pears in syrup until all pears are cooked.

6. Return all the cooked pears to the syrup. Cover the kettle and let stand in a cool place for 12 to 18 hours.

7. Pack pears into hot sterilized pint jars.

8. Remove spice bag from syrup. Heat syrup to boiling and pour over pears, leaving ¼ inch head space.

9. Seal and process pint jars 15 minutes in boiling water bath according to directions on page 26.

Tomato marmalade

4 quarts peeled tomatoes
3 oranges
2 lemons
16 cups sugar
1 tablespoon whole cloves

1. Cut tomatoes into chunks, squeezing a little juice from each tomato as you cut it up; otherwise you'll have to boil it out later.

2. Cut oranges and lemons in quarters then sliver, using both the peel and fruit.

3. In a large heavy kettle combine tomatoes with sugar, slivered oranges and lemons, and cloves, tied in a spice bag.

4. Cook slowly until thick. The length of time will vary greatly with the variety of tomato you are using and its juiciness. Stir frequently to prevent sticking.

5. Pour into hot sterilized jars and seal.

Apple marmalade

8 cups cooking apples, sliced
1½ cups water
5 cups sugar
2 tablespoons lemon juice
1 orange

1. Peel, core and thinly slice enough cooking apples to measure 8 cups of sliced fruit.

2. Bring water and sugar to a boil, stirring until all sugar is dissolved.

3. Add lemon juice, apples, and orange, thinly sliced and slivered. Boil rapidly until the mixture reaches 211 degrees.

4. Remove from heat, skim off the foam, ladle into eight sterilized half-pint jars, and seal.

Strawberry rhubarb jam

4 cups rhubarb, cut in ½-inch slices
8 cups sugar
8 cups strawberries, washed and hulled

The rhubarb takes on the flavor of the strawberries in this jam recipe.

1. Combine rhubarb with sugar, stir, and let stand overnight.

2. In the morning, simmer gently for 10 minutes.

3. Add strawberries and bring to a boil. Stir frequently until thick, about 10 minutes.

4. Ladle into hot sterilized jars and seal. Makes about five pints.

Pickled pears, with stems intact, simmer with lemons for a delicious and special treat.

Homemade syrups are easy to prepare and make a good breakfast even better. Shown here are apricot, maple, and berry.

Black chutney

1 pound Damson plums
  Water
2 cups dark corn syrup
½ cup cider vinegar
½ pound (1¼ cups) raisins
10 prunes, cooked, pitted and chopped
1 apple, peeled, cored, and chopped
½ teaspoon *each,* ground allspice, pepper, cloves, cardamon, and ginger
  Dash of cayenne

1. Cook plums with just enough water to keep fruit from burning until soft enough to remove pits.

2. Remove pits, return plums to kettle and add the remaining ingredients.

3. Stirring often, cook gently until thickened, about 30 minutes. Pack into hot sterilized jars, seal, and process in a boiling water bath for 20 minutes. (See page 26 for directions)

Fruit chutney

1 cup cranberry sauce
5 pounds tart apples, peeled, cored, and chopped
3 small onions, finely chopped
1 sweet red pepper, seeded and chopped
4 green peppers, seeded and chopped
  Juice of 2 lemons
2 cups cider vinegar
1 cup white raisins
1 cup brown sugar
1 tablespoon chopped, preserved or candied ginger
  Pinch *each* of cloves and cinnamon

1. Spoon cranberry sauce into a sieve to drain; reserve sauce.

2. Place cranberry juice in heavy kettle with the apples, onions, red pepper, green peppers, lemon juice, and vinegar. Stirring frequently, cook over low heat for 1½ hours.

3. Add the reserved cranberry sauce, raisins, sugar, ginger, cloves, and cinnamon; cook until thick, about 1 hour.

4. Pour into hot sterilized jars and seal.

Fruit syrups and others

Making syrup for waffles, pancakes, and toppings is easy and so nice to have handy. Years ago one made sugar syrups by putting plain sugar into a black iron skillet and cooking over a slow fire until it melted. The sugar was then covered with boiling water and allowed to simmer until it completely dissolved and the syrup became very thick. And presto, you had a very tasty caramel syrup.

Fruit syrups

Use this general fruit syrup recipe for Damson plums, black cherries, black and red currants, strawberries, raspberries, and loganberries. Cook the fruit in a very small amount of water until the juices begin to flow. Press with a wooden spoon or potato masher to help extract the juices. Pour mixture into a jelly bag and let drain overnight. If you're not that concerned about how clear your syrup is and if you want more quantity, put the pulp through a food mill instead of the jelly bag. To each 2½ cups juice add 1½ cups sugar. Bring it almost to a boil, stirring until the sugar dissolves. Pour into bottles and seal.

Homemade maple syrup . . . almost

Bring 2 cups sugar and 1 cup water to a boil and add ½ teaspoon commercial maple flavoring. It's that simple and sweet.

Rose petal syrup

4 cups rose petals
2 cups water
2 cups sugar
¼ teaspoon powdered cloves
  Red food coloring or beet juice

1. Simmer rose petals, water, sugar, and cloves for one hour.

2. Add a few drops of red food coloring or beet juice, until the color suits you.

3. Strain through a very fine sieve, bottle, and cap.

I store homemade syrups in soft drink bottles with screw-on caps and sometimes I put on caps with a bottle capper. Wash the bottles carefully with a bristly bottle brush. Rinse the bottles and lids, then boil in hot water for 10 minutes to insure sterilization. Pour the hot syrup all the way to the top of the bottles and cap each one as you fill it. I find it easier later, to pour syrup from a bottle than from a wider mouthed mason jar.

Cherry syrup

15 cups sour cherries
7½ cups sugar
3 cups light corn syrup

1. Bring sour cherries to a boil, stirring constantly; boil gently until tender, about 5 to 8 minutes.

2. Put through a food mill, then measure 7 cups of pulp.

3. Mix the pulp, sugar, and corn syrup and bring to a hard rolling boil for one minute, stirring constantly.

4. Pour into seven hot sterilized pint bottles and cap.

Prune-plum syrup

4 pounds ripe prune plums, pitted
1 cup water
5¾ cups sugar
2½ cups light corn syrup

1. Boil plums in water, stirring gently, for 5 to 8 minutes or until soft.

2. Put through a food mill and measure 5¼ cups fruit.

3. Combine fruit with sugar and corn syrup. Stir and bring to a boil; stirring constantly, boil 1 minute.

4. Pour into five hot sterilized pint bottles and cap.

Prune plums sometimes jell, depending on their ripeness. Don't worry if the plums misbehave, just place the bottle in a pan of hot water until it re-liquifies.

Loganberry syrup

8 cups loganberries
3½ cups sugar
1½ cups light corn syrup

1. Clean loganberries and heat until soft. If loganberries are not completely ripe, add a small amount of water to hasten softening.

2. Place in a jelly bag and drain overnight.

3. Place 3½ cups loganberry juice and sugar in a heavy kettle.

4. Mix in corn syrup and bring to a full boil; boil for 1 minute, stirring constantly.

5. Pour into hot sterilized bottles and cap.

Cinnamon syrup

4 cups apple juice
1 cup light corn syrup
½ cup red hot cinnamon candies
1 cinnamon stick

1. To home prepared or commercial apple juice, add corn syrup, cinnamon candies, cinnamon stick.

2. Cook until reduced in bulk by one-half (about 45 minutes).

3. Remove the cinnamon stick.

4. Bottle, and cap.

Grape syrup

Boil 1 cup grape juice or purée and 2 cups sugar for one minute, stirring constantly. Add 1 tablespoon lemon juice. Bottle, and cap.

Orange juice syrup

Boil 1 cup strained orange juice and 2 cups sugar for 1 minute. Add 2 tablespoons lemon juice. Bottle, and cap.

Apricot syrup

Mix 4 cups apricot purée, 1 cup water, 3 tablespoons lemon juice, and 4 cups sugar. Boil for 5 minutes. Skim, pour, into hot sterilized bottles, and cap.

Fruit butters

This recipe applies to apple, grape, peach, pear, or plum butters. In general you use 1 cup fruit pulp to ½ cup sugar. Spice to taste and cook slowly.

To make apple butter use tart cooking apples, not the sweet eating variety. Wash, quarter, and core the unpeeled fruit. Place in a heavy kettle with just enough water to prevent scorching. Cook until soft and press through a food mill.

For 16 cups apple purée, add 1 cup cider or cider vinegar, 8 cups sugar (half of this can be brown sugar), and 4 teaspoons cinnamon. Cook slowly, stirring frequently, until thick. This usually takes about 2 hours. If you try to hurry the process you could easily burn the mixture.

For an easier method, try cooking the fruit butter until thick in a roasting pan in a 250-300 degree oven. Stir occasionally. This way it needs little or no attention. You can also let it cook slowly in an electric crock pot. When fruit butter is thick, in about 2 to 2½ hours, pack in hot sterilized jars, and seal.

Candied fruits

Nearly everyone enjoys the taste of fresh candied fruits. They take several days to make, but only a few minutes per day. Be sure you store candied fruit in a cardboard box or in loose storage with waxed paper in between the layers. Do not store in an air tight can unless you want to liquidize the fruit for a specific fruit cake recipe. For longer storage, the rule is, the drier the better. Read ahead to the chapter on drying foods and adapt this for your candied products.

Candied citrus peel

I never seem to plan ahead to candy citrus peel. It just happens when we get a nice extra batch of fruit. Thick-skinned fruit with the least amount of white pith next to the skin is best for candying.

Carefully peel the fruit, leaving the peel in as large pieces as possible. You can eat the fruit but save the peelings in a plastic bag in the refrigerator until you have enough.

Use the skin of either 6 oranges or 3 grapefruit. Remove all the white area and cut the outer peel into strips. I cut ¼-inch strips, but you can choose your own size. Cover the strips with cold water and boil for 1 minute. Drain and repeat the process two more times. Then cook the peel slowly in a mixture of ½ cup water and 1 cup sugar until the syrup is absorbed. Remove one piece of peel at a time and roll in granulated sugar. Place on a rack to dry. The longer the drying time, the better the finished product.

Mexican preserved pumpkin

Remove the seeds from a pumpkin. Cut into strips, peel with a vegetable peeler, and cut into 1-inch cubes. Place the cubes in a solution of 4 tablespoons lime and 1 gallon of water. Be sure it is well covered and let stand for 12 hours. Drain and wash thoroughly. Weigh pumpkin and mix with an equal weight of sugar. Let stand for one hour.

When the juice begins to flow, place over a low heat and cook very slowly until the pumpkin is dark brown and transparent. Remove the cubes from the syrup and place on waxed paper in the sun. Dry until no moisture shows, from 5 to 7 days.

Preserved ginger root

This is used in many oriental recipes and adds a most unusual flavor to many dishes. For each one pound of peeled and cleaned ginger root, begin with slightly more than a pound. Ginger has a pungent taste and should be cut into small (½-inch) cubes.

Soak the cubed ginger in cold water for 15 minutes, drain. Pour over fresh water, boil for 5 minutes, and drain. Repeat two more times until the ginger is very tender. Drain and cool.

Weigh the ginger again. For each pound of ginger, place 1¼ pounds of sugar and 1 cup water in a pan. Boil until the sugar is dissolved. Add the ginger, remove from heat, and let stand for 24 hours. Remove ginger from the syrup with a slotted spoon; reheat syrup just to boiling. Return ginger to the syrup and let stand for 48 hours. Remove the ginger and pack in small jars. Reheat the syrup again and pour over the ginger. Cover the jars. Let stand for 2 weeks before using so the ginger will absorb as much syrup as possible.

Candied figs

3 cups sugar
3 cups water
5 pounds washed figs

1. Boil sugar and water, stirring until sugar is dissolved.

2. Add figs (stemming is up to you), cover, and simmer gently for one hour.

3. Remove from heat and let stand for 24 hours.

4. Simmer very gently again for one hour, and then let stand for 48 hours.

5. Uncover and simmer until almost all of syrup is absorbed, watching carefully so the figs do not scorch.

6. Place figs on a cloth and dry outside in the sun for 4 to 5 days. Bring them in at night if the weather is damp or foggy.

7. When dry, roll in fine sugar or chopped walnuts.

Quince cheese

Actually this isn't really a cheese but a sweet and flavorful preserved fruit. Wash, quarter, and core five pounds of unpeeled quince. Cover with a small amount of water, and cook until soft. Press through a food mill. Measure, and for each cup of purée, use 1 cup of sugar. Cook slowly for one hour, or until thick and dark red, stirring frequently.

Pour into a greased shallow pan or little candy molds and cool. Leave in the container and dry in the sun for several days. Turn out of molds and turn the fruit to dry all sides. When quite dry slice into ⅛-inch thick slices. Dry a final time and roll in super fine sugar. Quince cheese makes an elegant dessert.

Honeyed fruit rinds

Cut citrus rinds into strips and remove all the white pith. Cover with water and 1 teaspoon salt to each cup

Brandied and yeast fermented fruits are good keepers and improve with age; always appreciated during the winter when fresh fruit is hard to come by. (See recipes pages 34-35)

of rind. Boil for 30 minutes and drain. Boil again in fresh water until tender and drain. Pour in ¾ cup honey for each cup of rind. Simmer slowly until the rind is clear, about 45 minutes. Watch carefully as mixture is thick and burns easily.

Place the rind on waxed paper. Let dry for 2 to 3 days and then roll in fine sugar. This recipe differs from the others in the use of honey instead of sugar.

Cactus candy

1 cactus leaf
3 cups sugar
½ cup water
2 tablespoons orange juice
1 tablespoon lemon juice

1. Remove the spines from a piece of cactus leaf, peel, and cut into ½-inch thick slices.

2. Cover with water, and soak overnight.

3. Drain and cut the strips into cubes.

4. Add sugar, water, orange juice, and lemon juice, then cook until the syrup is absorbed. Just before the syrup is completely absorbed, you can add food coloring if desired. Watch carefully while it cooks.

5. Dry the pieces on racks. The drier it becomes, the longer it will keep.

Candied pineapple

1 large (No. 2½ can) sliced pineapple
2 cups sugar
⅓ cup light corn syrup

1. Drain pineapple reserving the juice.

2. Pat pineapple slices dry with paper toweling.

3. Place the reserved juice, sugar, and corn syrup in a wide skillet, and bring to a boil.

4. Arrange the pineapple slices in a single layer in the skillet simmering until the slices are clear, about 15 minutes. Turn over halfway through cooking.

5. Place on racks and let stand until very dry.

Candied cranberries

1 cup large, perfect cranberries
1 cup sugar
1 cup water
Granulated sugar

1. Prick each cranberry several times with a sterilized needle.

2. Place sugar and water in a pot, cover, and boil for 3 minutes to remove any sugar crystals.

3. Remove the lid and cook, without stirring, to 238 degrees F.

4. Remove from heat and add the cranberries. Let stand for about 5 minutes or until translucent.

5. Drain and dry cranberries on waxed paper.

6. When almost dry roll the cranberries in granulated sugar for a nice frosting.

Candied kumquats

4 cups kumquats
5 cups water
2 cups sugar
⅛ teaspoon cream of tartar

Candied kumquats are a gourmet delicacy and a great favorite of ours.

1. Wash kumquats and prick a hole in the stem end of each.

2. Cover with 4 cups cold water and bring slowly to a boil. Simmer until tender, about 10 minutes.

3. Drain.

4. Bring to a boil 1 cup water.

5. Stir in sugar and cream of tartar, and boil to 238 degrees F.

6. Add kumquats and cook slowly for 10 minutes.

7. Remove the kumquats with a slotted spoon and drain on a rack.

8. When cool, roll in granulated sugar and let dry.

Candied fruit from canned fruit

For this you can use home canned fruit or canned fruit that you buy. If you use home canned, be sure the fruit is not overripe and soft.

Drain a 1-pound can (2 cups) of fruit and measure the syrup. Add enough water to it to make 1¼ cups liquid and place in a pan with 1 cup sugar, or if possible, ½ cup sugar and ½ cup glucose. Heat, stirring constantly, until the sugar dissolves. Bring to a boil, then pour over the fruit. Use a plate to weight the fruit down and keep it under the syrup. Let stand for 24 hours.

The next day, strain the syrup into a pan and add ¼ cup sugar. Heat and stir until sugar is dissolved. Bring to a boil, pour over fruit, and let stand another 24 hours.

Repeat this process two more times, (you will have done it a total of four times), but the last time add only 3 tablespoons sugar and check the syrup for consistency. Pour a small amount of the hot syrup onto a chilled plate. It should be as thick as honey. If it is not, repeat the process a fifth time, this time again adding 3 table-spoons sugar to the syrup. Once the syrup is thick enough, let the sub-merged and covered fruit sit for four more days.

Finally, drain the fruit and place on a rack in a warm place, such as in the sun or a cooling oven. The temperature should not exceed 120 degrees F. At this point you should thoroughly dry the fruit (consult the chapter on drying). To add a crystal-line finish, dip each piece of dried fruit quickly in boiling water and then roll in super fine granulated sugar. Apricots are nice this way.

Be sure you don't start out with mushy fruit. Don't let the amount of time involved discourage you. Actually, the fruit is "resting" most of the time. You only need time to bring the liquid to a boil and that's it for that day. When you see the beautifully candied fruit, you'll appreciate the real simplicity of this recipe.

Mock maraschino cherries

An easy recipe for beginners. Use Royal Ann cherries; the big secret is to make sure they're not too ripe.

4¼ pounds 'Royal Ann' cherries
2 tablespoons salt
1 teaspoon alum
1 quart water
3 cups water
4½ cups sugar
1 one-ounce bottle red food coloring
1 ounce almond extract
Juice of one lemon, strained
1 teaspoon imitation raspberry extract, optional
A few drops rose extract, optional

1. Pit cherries carefully and soak overnight in a brine made of salt, alum, and 1 quart water.

2. The following day wash the cherries until the salt taste is gone.

3. Bring 3 cups water, sugar, and food coloring just to a boil.

4. Add the cherries, remove from heat, and let stand 24 hours.

5. Next day bring the cherries and syrup just to a boil, adding the almond extract and lemon juice. (At this point you can add 1 teaspoon imitation raspberry extract and a few drops of rose extract. This step is optional.)

6. Pack the hot cherries and syrup in small hot sterilized jars and seal. Use baby food jars, or any other tiny container. I use most of my mara-schino cherries as a garnish for tapioca pudding. It is an old-fashioned item, but very popular in families with cows and a surplus of daily milk. With or without your own cow, the cherries will disappear rapidly.

Tutti frutti or the brandy crock

In colonial times as fruits came into season they were stored in crockery or stoneware jars with a pleasant amount of spirits added. This practice hap-pily has been revived. As the fruits slowly ferment, the spirits keep them from spoiling. The finished product is delicious served over puddings, plain cake, and especially ice cream.

There is a great variety in old recipes for brandied or crocked fruit. Some call for brandy, rum, or bourbon, while others call for a yeast starter. The fruit is generally sweetened with sugar, though some older cookbooks suggest adding a few lemon slices to cut the sweetness or to use honey in place of sugar. Try several, or make adaptations, to see what your family likes. Some recipes recommend wait-ing three months to taste. You can taste after a week, enjoy, and know that it will be that much better with each passing day.

Crocked fruit

This recipe calls for a combination of fresh, dried, and canned fruit, and makes the greatest assortment pos-sible. Use fresh peaches, seedless grapes, pineapple, nectarines, plums, apples, and a few strawberries. The flavor of the strawberries is nice though they tend to disintegrate when stored too long.

Peel and pit fresh fruit if necessary as you use it. You can use dried fruit such as pitted prunes, apricots, raisins, figs, and pitted dates. Most canned fruit can be used including peaches, pears, pineapple, apricots, cherries, and maraschino cherries. Walnut and pecan halves can also be used. Cut any fruits you use in rather large pieces. If you cut the pieces too small, you will end up with purée.

To begin the crock, prepare and cut up a batch of fruit—either one kind or a variety. Weigh the fruit and mix it with an equal weight of sugar. If you don't have a scale, use ¾ cup sugar for each 1 cup of fresh or dried fruit. Use ⅓ cup sugar for each 1 cup of drained canned fruit. Eliminate the sugar when you use nuts.

Mix the sugar and fruit and let stand for one hour. Place it in the crock, and just barely cover with brandy, rum, bourbon, or any spirit of your choice. Cover the crock tightly and store in a cool dry place. Stir once a day for the first few days.

As new fruits come into season, or when you want to add more dried or canned fruit, mix the fruit with sugar using the original proportions. Let the mixture stand for one hour to dissolve the sugar before adding to the crock. Stir once a day for a few days each time you add a batch of fruit to the crock. Because the fruit makes its own alcoholic juices, you won't need to add additional spirits unless the fruit is not covered with liquid. Then you may need to add a little.

Let the mixture stand for as long as possible before using. Wait at least one week the first time and at least one week after the addition of each new fruit. Stir before using. Use over homemade vanilla ice cream for a nice holiday treat.

Brandy crock

There are seven fruits in this brandied mixture. You might start it with pine-apple and strawberries. Mix 1 quart of cubed pineapple and 1 quart of hulled strawberries with 9 cups sugar. Let stand for one hour to dissolve sugar, then place in a stoneware crock and add I quart brandy. As each fruit comes into season, add 1 quart each of the following with 4½ cups sugar per quart of fruit—pitted cherries, peeled and pitted apricots, rasp-berries, currants, and gooseberries. Let each fruit mixture stand until sugar dissolves before adding to the crock.

Store in a cool place, stirring once a day, until the last of the fruit is added. This crock contains the softer fruits and has more of a dessert-like appearance.

Brandied fruit mélange

This isn't a typical fermented fruit, but it has a nice flavor spiced with brandy. It is important not to overcook each individual fruit.

12 plums, firm and ripe
6 peaches, firm and ripe
1 pound seedless grapes
2 cups sugar
1½ cups water
6 cinnamon sticks
Brandy

1. Prick plums in several places with a sterilized needle.

2. Peel, halve, and pit peaches.

3. Stem grapes.

4. In a large kettle, mix sugar, water, and cinnamon sticks.

5. Stirring, cook until sugar dissolves.

6. Poach the plums in the simmering syrup for four minutes. Add the peaches and grapes and continue cooking for five minutes.

7. Remove fruit with a slotted spoon and pack into six hot sterilized jars.

8. Place one cinnamon stick in each jar.

9. Bring the syrup to a boil and pour over fruit, filling jars three-fourths full.

10. Add brandy to within ½-inch of the top and seal. The amount of brandy used won't affect the recipe, so you can use a little more or less if you wish.

Yeast fermented fruit

Mix together ¾ cup drained canned peaches, ¾ cup drained canned pineapple cubes, six maraschino cherries, 1½ cups sugar, and one package active dry yeast. Place in a crock and cover loosely. The first day, stir several times, then stir once a day for two weeks. Keep at room temperature.

After two weeks remove 1 cup of the fermented fruit to use as a starter for a new batch (you can eat what is left). To the starter add ¾ cup *each* drained peaches and cubed pineapple and six maraschino cherries. Add only 1 cup sugar. Let stand for one week before using. When you need another batch, steal more starter from the original crock, and add new fruit and sugar.

This recipe does not include spirits, but since the sugar, yeast, and fruit make alcohol, don't use this recipe if you want to avoid alcoholic products.

On preserving vegetables

A variety of ways to preserve some of the more unusual vegetables, including canning, brining, and marinating.

Artichokes

Artichokes are my favorite vegetable, relish and treat. We are fortunate to live near Castroville, a little town in California about 70 miles south of San Francisco which calls itself the Artichoke Capital of the World. Here I can buy a giant bag of 50 of the tiniest chokes for $1.50. You may have to pay more where you live, but if you find a good buy on small artichokes you might want to put some away for future pleasure.

Wash artichokes, cut off the stem and one inch of tops and peel off any discolored leaves. Soak two minutes in water with a little lemon juice to prevent discoloration. To boil artichokes put in a large kettle of salted water, cover, and steam for 30 minutes to one hour, depending on the size. When you can pull a leaf out easily the vegetable is done.

If you find the tiny baby artichokes, steam 50 at a time and eat part of them with homemade mayonnaise or melted butter. What you don't eat marinate for another meal.

Marinated baby artichokes

1 teaspoon salt
¼ teaspoon pepper, freshly ground
A dash of cayenne
½ teaspoon dry mustard
1 tablespoon Worcestershire
1 tablespoon minced onion
1 clove garlic, minced
2 tablespoons vinegar
⅓ cup olive oil, or salad oil

Combine salt, pepper, cayenne, dry mustard, Worcestershire, minced onion, garlic, vinegar, and olive oil or salad oil. Pour over tiny cooked artichokes and marinate in the refrigerator overnight.

To can artichokes

Since artichokes are low in acid, you need to add an acid solution and can them in a steam pressure canner. I generally can only the most beautiful and uniform small artichokes. Clean and trim artichokes. Precook

An inside view of an artichoke reveals symmetrical perfection, but gives little idea of its delicious flavor.

for 5 minutes in a mixture of ¾ cup vinegar for each gallon of water. Drain. Pack into hot jars and seal. Cover with a boiling brine made from ¾ cup lemon juice or vinegar and 3 tablespoons salt to one gallon of water. Fill to within ½ inch of tops of jars. Cook in a steam pressure canner. Process pints and quarts 25 minutes at 10 pounds pressure (see page 27 for complete directions).

To freeze artichokes

Wash and trim small baby artichokes. Blanch in a mixture of ½ cup lemon juice to two quarts water. Cook 3 to 5 minutes (or 10 minutes for medium sized artichokes). Drain, chill, package, and freeze.

French fried artichoke hearts

Thaw a dozen small artichokes, cut in halves or quarters, and remove chokes. Dip in a batter of one egg, ¼ cup milk, ½ cup flour, ¼ teaspoon baking powder, and salt and pepper to taste. Cook in deep fat 370 degrees for 2 to 3 minutes. Drain on paper toweling.

Brining vegetables

Brining vegetables lengthens their storage life and imparts a good flavor, relished by pickle lovers.

Brined products have a refreshing taste and the saltiness provides a good contrast, especially nice with a heavy meal.

Small whole cucumbers, small onions, green beans, tiny carrots, sections of celery stalks, cauliflower pieces, and small ears of corn on the cob, cut in sections, can be preserved in a brine of three pounds pickling salt, 2 cups vinegar, and one gallon of water. Use at least 2 cups of brine per one pound of cleaned and prepared vegetables. After mixing well, pack an assortment into glass jars, cover completely with the brine, and seal. Or you can store the vegetables in the brine in a crock. Keep in a cool place for storage.

To serve, remove the vegetables you want, drain, and rinse off the brine, cover with clear water, and parboil for 3 to 4 minutes. Drain and cook in a small amount of water until tender.

Salt brined peppers

You can store peppers by salt brining. There is no particular flavor change so you can begin to use the peppers as soon as you wish. Remove the stems and seeds from a good quantity of freshly picked green peppers. Pack loosely in a crock or gallon jar. Cover with a brine made from one pound pickling salt to two quarts of water. Heat just enough to dissolve salt and then cool before pouring over peppers.

Be sure peppers are completely submerged in the brine. Fill the air space between the green peppers and the jar lid with crumpled cellophane to keep peppers "down under." Store in a cool cellar. Freshen in several changes of cold water before using. I find that they have a good color, crispness and are excellent in cooking. I use them for stuffed peppers, a real treat in mid-winter. When stuffing, do not oversalt the meat or rice. There always seems to be a little salt remaining from the brine.

Grape leaves

You can preserve grape leaves to make an interesting Armenian dish called Sarma. Early in the season when the grape leaves are tender, gather leaves that are uniform in size. Heat 2 teaspoons salt and 1 quart water in a large kettle. Add grape leaves for 30 seconds. Drain, then form into loose rolls and pack in pint jars. Add 1 cup lemon juice or 2½ teaspoons citric acid to 1 quart water. Bring to a boil, then cover rolls of leaves in jars. Seal. Process in boiling water bath for 15 minutes according to directions on page 26.

Sarma

Prepare this mixture for the filling of stuffed grape leaves.

1 pound ground beef or ground lamb, or a mixture of both
2 onions, finely chopped
¼ cup uncooked rice
¼ cup chopped parsley
2 tablespoons fresh mint, chopped
Salt and pepper to taste
Grape leaves
2 cups canned tomatoes
1 tablespoon lemon juice

1. Mix together meat, onions, rice, parsley, mint, and salt and pepper to taste.

2. Remove grape leaves from one jar, wash in hot water, and carefully separate. Spread leaves out on work surface, rib side up; cut off stems.

3. Place 1 to 1½ teaspoons meat filling in the center of each leaf, fold like an envelope, and roll up.

4. Place a few unfilled grape leaves or a few sprigs parsley in the bottom of a heavy kettle; top with layers of filled grape leaves.

5. Pour in canned tomatoes, lemon juice, and enough water to barely cover. Weight down with an inverted plate.

6. Cover pan and simmer for 1 hour. Let cool a few minutes before arranging on serving platter.

Grape leaves, picked when young and tender, are preserved for future use for the Armenian dish Sarma

The Korean dish, Kim Chee, is made principally from cabbage, garlic, and hot red peppers. In Korea the ingredients are put into glazed pots and buried in the ground for the winter. In spring, after the snow has melted, the pots are retrieved; by this time the ingredients have fermented into quite a spicy side dish. Also pictured is a contemporary "pickle pot" good for making Kim Chee and similar dishes.

Vegetable jardiniere

5 cups water
4 cups carrots, crinkle-cut
3 pounds green beans, cut diagonally
6 cucumbers, scored and sliced
Brine:
3 cups vinegar
2 tablespoons dill seed
1 tablespoon dill weed
1 tablespoon salt
1 teaspoon pepper, freshly ground
4 cloves garlic, crushed
  Fresh dill flowers

1. Boil the water.

2. Add crinkle-cut carrots, green beans, and cucumbers. Simmer the vegetables until lightly done, then remove from cooking liquid.

3. Arrange vegetables in separate layers in six sterilized jars.

4. Mix the cooking liquid with the vinegar, dill seed, dill weed, salt, freshly ground pepper, garlic, and dill flowers. Bring to a boil to dissolve salt, then cool the liquid.

5. Pour over the vegetables, arranging a dill spray in each jar and seal.

6. Process 20 minutes in boiling water bath according to directions on page 26.

This recipe can be especially attractive if you cut and arrange the vegetables carefully.

Janet's Nappa cabbage (Kim Chee)

Wash and drain Nappa cabbage, sometimes called Chinese or celery cabbage. Use about 1½ pounds of the stiffer part of the cabbage, reserving the lettucy part for another use. Cut the stems and ends into pieces 2 inches by ½ inch. Let stand dry overnight to wilt.

Dissolve 4 tablespoons salt in 1½ cups warm water. Add ½ teaspoon peppercorns (use Szechuen peppercorns if available), several whole dried red chili peppers, and 1 teaspoon dry sherry. Pour the brine and the cabbage into a jar or crock. Cover with an inverted plate, weight down, and let stand for four days. Remove from brine and taste. If it is too salty, rinse in cold water before serving. Store at 70 degrees on the kitchen counter: vegetables are cured when they are pale and almost translucent, like good sauerkraut. The vegetable will continue to ferment at room temperature. When you are pleased with the taste, refrigerate.

After six weeks, the vegetables may develop a musty flavor, so consume early. You can re-use the brine. Add 1 more teaspoon salt to the brine and pour it over a combination of 2-inch pieces of carrot sticks, green beans, celery sticks, and Nappa cabbage slices. Pickled Nappa cabbage is a nice salad substitute or a party hors d'oeuvre. Serve as you would a pickle or relish.

Make Korean Kim Chee the same way, but triple the amount of hot red peppers and add several garlic cloves.

Japanese pickles

2 cucumbers
4 carrots
1 daikon (Japanese radish)
4 small white turnips
4 Japanese eggplants (the small narrow variety)
  Salt

1. Peel and slice the cucumbers, carrots, daikon, and white turnips. Slice unpeeled Japanese egg plants.

2. Arrange sliced vegetables in a crock or jar, sprinkling a little salt between the layers.

3. Cover with a plate and rock weight. Ferment for four days.

To serve, remove from brine and serve with soy sauce or soy sauce mixed with a little vinegar.

Dill crock

I plant fresh dill all season, save the dill seed, and have fresh dill to use in a nice dill crock.

For the vegetables, use green beans and wax beans (parboil 3 minutes before adding to the crock), raw cauliflower sections, sliced onions and leeks, green pepper strips, sliced green tomatoes and cucumbers, Jerusalem artichokes, and any other vegetable of your choice. In a crock, alternate layers of vegetables with a seasoned mixture of fresh dill, garlic cloves, and a few small red hot peppers. Heat ¾ cup pickling salt, 10 cups water, and ¼ cup vinegar long enough to dissolve salt. Cool, then pour brine over vegetables.

Cover, weight down, and let stand in a cool place for 2 weeks. Remove scum daily. Remove vegetables from brine and pack in hot sterilized jars. Heat ½ cup salt, 4 cups vinegar, and 1 gallon water. Pour over vegetables in the jars and seal. Process in a boiling water bath for 15 minutes according to directions on page 26.

Salsa

2 pounds fresh chilis
1 pound onions
5 pounds tomatoes
2 teaspoons salt
½ teaspoon pepper
⅓ cup lemon juice

Choose your own variety of fresh chilis for this salsa, depending on how hot you want it to be.

1. Wash, seed, and chop fresh chilis. Peel and chop onions. Peel and chop tomatoes.

2. Mix vegetables with salt, pepper, and lemon juice.

3. Pack cold in hot sterilized jars, seal, and process in a boiling water bath for 10 minutes. Or bring to a boil and pack hot into hot sterilized jars and seal at once. No further processing is necessary. Makes 6 pints.

Relishes

Relishes put zing into meals, are easy to make, and wonderful to have on hand. Often you can turn an over-supply of food from your garden into a relish.

Most relishes are packed hot in sterilized jars, sealed at once, and need no further processing. Some recipes however recommend processing in a boiling water bath. *Always* follow the recipe recommendation.

Relishes are usually high in acid as they contain a large amount of vinegar which helps prevent spoilage. Authorities recommend that you do not use home made vinegars to prepare relishes or pickles since it is difficult at home to accurately test the acidity content.

Green tomato relish

6 quarts green tomatoes, quartered
3 quarts small onions, quartered, and peeled
1 quart sweet green pepper, chopped
1 sweet red pepper, chopped
10 teaspoons salt
8 cups sugar
4 cups cider vinegar
4 cups water

Just before the first fall frost, pick small green tomatoes. They make a marvelous relish that our family likes on meat sandwiches.

1. In a large heavy kettle place quartered green tomatoes, quartered small onions, green pepper, red pepper, salt, sugar, cider vinegar, and water.

2. Stirring occasionally, cook gently until onions are clear.

3. Pack hot into hot sterilized jars and seal at once. Process in boiling water bath 5 minutes. Makes 12 pints.

Zucchini relish

Here's a good way to enjoy the harvest of the prolific zucchini plant. Use the coarse blade of the food chopper to grind all the vegetables.

4 cups ground zucchini
3 cups ground carrots
4½ cups ground onions
1½ cups ground red or green peppers
¼ cup salt
2¼ cups vinegar
¾ cup sugar
1 tablespoon celery seed
¾ teaspoon dry mustard

1. In a large kettle combine ground zucchini, ground carrots, ground onions, ground red or green pepper, salt, vinegar, sugar, celery seed, and dry mustard.

2. Cook for 20 minutes or until vegetables are crisp tender.

A Scandinavian specialty, pickled herring, is easy to prepare at home. Most of the herring available in this country has been preserved in a salt brine, making it necessary to soak and rinse the fish in cold water. Sweet red onion, pickling spices, vinegar, and the herring itself, are the principal ingredients. A brine of vinegar, water, and a little sugar is poured over the fish; a few days in the refrigerator and you have a taste treat.

3. While still hot, pack into hot sterilized jars, seal, and process in a boiling water bath for 20 minutes. Makes 4 to 5 pints. See page 26.

Horseradish

Horseradish is a novel product to have in your garden, is easy to grow, and is the spirited component of many gourmet sauces and dishes. It gives a nice sharpness to boiled meats, especially the corned varieties.

To use the roots, wash carefully, scrubbing with a stiff brush. Peel with a vegetable peeler, trimming off the rough spots. When you get down to the nice white meat, grind using the fine blade of the food chopper or finely grate it. You can also whirl it in the blender. You may have to add a few drops of water.

I think the best way is to peel and grate horseradish as you need it. Wrap the remainder of the unpeeled root and store in the refrigerator. For longer storage, freeze pieces of the whole root or little packets of grated horseradish. Although they are easy enough to grow, it's nice to have a never ending supply.

Mayonnaise-whipped cream sauce

This sharp sauce is especially delightful on sandwiches.

    3 tablespoons mayonnaise
    ½ teaspoon dry mustard
    1 tablespoon vinegar
    2 tablespoons grated horseradish
    ¼ teaspoon marjoram or basil
      A few grains of cayenne
    ½ cup whipping cream

1. Combine mayonnaise, dry mustard, vinegar, grated horseradish, marjoram or basil, and the cayenne.

2. Whip the whipping cream.

3. Fold seasonings into cream.

Sour cream horseradish for prime rib dinners

Blend thick sour cream, freshly grated horseradish, and a little lemon juice. Proportions depend on your taste. You'll find this sauce in restaurants served with prime rib roast cuts.

Hot horseradish

    Fresh horseradish
    ½ cup white vinegar
    ½ teaspoon salt

1. Wash, peel, and grate or chop in blender, enough horseradish to fill 1 cup.

2. Add white vinegar and salt. Mix well, and pack into tiny sterilized jars. Cover and refrigerate.

3. Use sparingly in recipes calling for horseradish. This is hot, hot, hot.

Fresh horseradish sauce

    ½ cup freshly grated horseradish
    2 teaspoons prepared mustard
    2 teaspoons vinegar
    1 teaspoon salt
    ½ teaspoon pepper
    1 teaspoon sugar
    4 tablespoons cream

Combine and heat freshly grated horseradish, mustard, vinegar, salt, pepper, sugar, and cream. Do not boil. Serve with sliced beef or ham.

Pickled Herring

Uncooked fish is common fare in much of the world, but many Americans are unaccustomed to this nutritious food. Here's a recipe for pickled herring, and if you don't tell anyone it's raw fish, you'll have a lot more takers. Makes a delicious hors-d'oeuvre when served on rye crackers.

    24 salt herring
    2 sweet red onions, thinly sliced
    ⅓ cup pickling spice
    2 bay leaves
      White vinegar
      Water
      Sugar

1. Soak the salt herring in cold water for three hours. It is advisable to change the water once or twice during this soaking. Drain.

2. Cut the herring down the backbone and cut into bite-sized pieces.

3. Place the herring, onions, and spices into a small crock. Alternate layers of fish and onions, while dispersing the spices throughout.

4. Mix a brine of 2½ parts of water to 1 part vinegar. For each cup of vinegar you use add 1½ tablespoons sugar. Stir to dissolve sugar and pour over herring, making sure there's enough brine to cover the fish. Add bay leaves to the crock.

5. Cover and refrigerate for at least 48 hours, the longer the fish marinate the better the flavor. Stir before using. Will keep indefinitely in the refrigerator.

The freezer...

A modern appliance that brought new ways to the old tradition of "putting food by."

Where to find it...

In addition to the books listed under Canning, try these:

Farm Journal Canning and Freezing
edited by Nichols — $9.95 revised
Doubleday and Co.
Garden City, NY 11530

Stocking Up — $12.95 revised
$14.95 deluxe edition
Editors of Rodale Press, Inc.
Emmaus, PA 10849

The following cookbooks contain recipes especially for freezing:

The Cook It and Freeze It. $3.95
by Margaret Reeds Murphy,
Hawthorne Books, Inc. N.Y.

For information on food choppers and sausage stuffers write to:

KitchenAid Division—
Electric Housewares
The Hobart Mfg. Co.
Troy, Ohio 45373

◁

One of the easiest ways to keep a freezer inventory is to keep track of "deposits and withdrawals" with a grease pencil right on the freezer door.

There is nothing quite as satisfying as looking at a well-stocked freezer—except the pleasure of dipping into the frozen harvest and enjoying it year 'round.

Today's freezer is truly one of the great modern conveniences. Not only does it provide the most efficient and safest way to store food, but it ensures a good selection of foods at all times and allows a certain flexibility not found in other methods of food preservation. The one rule to remember, though, is *use the food, don't just collect it.*

Although it sounds a little strange, you can make the most of your freezer if you compare it to a checking account—it serves you best only if you make continual deposits and withdrawals.

The swing of the seasons

During the peak of the harvest, deposits may be heavy as fruits and vegetables from your garden or produce stand come into season. Some may be immediately turned into pie fillings or casseroles, but if you are too busy at the time, the freezer can serve as a "storage bin" for bulk items until you decide how to use the produce at a later, quieter time.

Many baked goods and cooked entrées freeze well. You may deposit more of these items in the fall for future enjoyment during the holiday seasons. In the middle of winter you may have the time to prepare the soups and entrées that require longer preparation and cooking time. With a little advance planning the ingredients needed for these more time-consuming dishes will be the ones you stored in bulk during the summer. A rainy day may inspire you to grind some grain, and turn out several batches of bread—one loaf to enjoy now, the others to freeze.

You'll get the maximum enjoyment from the "deposits" in your freezer, *only* if you use them up. Somehow the frozen strawberries, which were so delicious all winter long, never taste quite as good after the first fresh berries ripen on the vine, and asparagus from the freezer never seems quite as fresh when the first shoots are pushing through the ground.

About freezers

A chest freezer retains the cold best, but an upright freezer is more convenient for storage of items and takes up less floor space. A manual defrost freezer uses less energy than an automatic defrost model and the original cost is much less, though you do need to defrost once or twice a year.

I've read that the average American consumes about 70 pounds of frozen food a year. You can figure how far from the average you are and plan accordingly. A 9-cubic foot freezer holds approximately 325 pounds of food, and an 11-cubic foot freezer holds 385 pounds, a 15-cubic foot freezer holds 525 pounds, and a 22-cubic foot holds 770 pounds. It's up to you to make the most of your freezer's cubic feet. Well-wrapped, compact, and carefully stacked packages allow you to maximize your freezer space.

The main functions of a freezer are to preserve quality, extend seasonal harvests, and prevent spoilage, (actually freezing does not kill bacteria, but simply stops its growth).

These are some basic rules: Blanch vegetables per instructions, wrap all foods carefully, seal out all air, and label packages with an indelible pen or grease pencil.

The food stored in your freezer has a definite freezer life. Here is where an inventory is most helpful. Note what you are storing, and where it is in the freezer. Without an inventory many of the advantages of the freezer are nullified.

Temperature control

It's a good idea to periodically check the temperature of your freezer. An inexpensive thermometer will do the job, and the results are sometimes surprising. The general recommendation is to keep the freezer at zero degrees, or minus 10, if possible. For every degree above zero, food storage time is reduced.

In a power outage, a full freezer can remain frozen up to 3 days if the gasket is in good condition and the door is kept completely closed. If the power should remain out for more than three days, dry ice can be used to keep the food frozen. It's worth the time to locate a dry ice distributor *before* the power suddenly evaporates; ice cream dealers or a cold storage warehouse are likely sources. If dry ice is not available, it's possible that a locker plant would temporarily store your food in an emergency.

If the power goes out in your freezer, the top packages will begin to thaw first. If they are close to 40 degrees, and contain ice crystals, only the quality will be lost. Dispose of any questionable looking food, or any food which has a disagreeable odor.

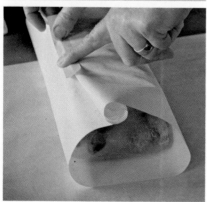

An easy way to freeze fish is to freeze them whole, in a block of ice.

1. Lay cleaned fish in a suitable container and cover with water. Freeze until solid.

2. Run just enough warm water over the container so the entire block will come out.

3. Wrap the frozen fish block in freezer paper and tape. Return to freezer until needed.

4. When you want to use the fish run lukewarm water over the block.

Packaging

A freezer is only as good as the food inside. The food is only as good as the wrapping material and procedure. It is false economy to save money on freezer papers.

If you have an automatic defrost freezer, you must be especially careful in wrapping the food since the dry air can cause freezer burn more rapidly than in a manual defrost freezer.

I buy a giant roll of coated freezer paper from our local locker plant operator, and have a pipe rigged up to hold it above my work area. To avoid extra aggravation I use a cutter to snap off the paper automatically. For sealing, masking tape is both effective and inexpensive. It also provides a firm surface for labeling. I always have plenty of plastic wrap on hand, as well.

I wrap the meat, for example, first with a firm layer of plastic wrap, tape it, and then rewrap it with coated paper.

Double plastic bags are also useful. Remember to wrap a padding around any sharp corners or bones. Don't be concerned if your own packaged meats are not trimmed as squarely as they are at the meat counter.

✓Aluminum foil and commercial plastic containers with tight fitting lids are excellent for packaging.

✓A one half-pound margarine tub holds exactly 1 cup and can be used for purées, and bits and dabs of things.

✓Wide-mouthed glass canning jars are also excellent. However, when using glass containers in the freezer be sure and leave at least 1-inch head-space for expansion or the jar will crack.

✓Cookies and crackers can be stored in coffee cans with the plastic lids.

When packaging something liquid in a plastic container, such as a purée or lemon juice, don't forget to leave head-space for expansion in freezing. If there is no room, the lid will pop off as the container freezes and air will seep inside.

Freezing tips

I've found the following tips handy sooner or later.

✓Store small packs of grated coconut, grated cheese, bread crumbs, blanched almonds, snipped parsley, and chopped nuts.

✓Frozen candles keep their shape longer, burn brighter, and won't drip.

✓Nothing bothers me more than to watch summer iced coffee turn into a luke-warm drink. Freeze leftover coffee into cubes and use in iced coffee to retain flavor.

✓Freezing will keep brown sugar and marshmallows soft.

✓Cheese can be frozen, although hard cheese tends to be crumbly unless grated.

✓If you plan to freeze cream sauces and gravies, be sure the fat and flour are thoroughly combined during preparation. This will reduce curdling during thawing. Stir sauces to regain smoothness.

✓Use pure vanilla when freezing baked products. The artificial variety sometimes develops an off-flavor.

✓For those impatient among us, nuts in the shell will open more easily after being frozen.

✓Stuffed baked potatoes can be individually wrapped for reheating.

✓Homemade pasta is messy to make, so double the batch. Liberally flour the still fresh, but thoroughly dry, pasta to prevent sticking, then freeze.

✓German cabbage rolls, chilis, curries, and most casseroles freeze well.

✓In freezing fatty fish such as tuna or salmon, dip the meat in a solution of 2 teaspoons ascorbic acid and 1 quart water, for 20 seconds, to prevent darkening and rancidity.

✓Leftover meats can be cubed and frozen for use in a big meat pie.

✓For stir-fry Oriental dishes, you can cut paper thin slices of meat if you begin cutting while the meat is still partially frozen.

✓Salted meats such as ham and bacon do not keep as long as other products, so rotate them more frequently. Home-cured pork meat is not as salty and stores much longer in the home freezer.

✓Sesame and poppy seeds, wheat germ, lentils, and beans can also be stored in the freezer. A week or two in frozen storage also decreases chances of weevil contamination. Once out of the freezer, store the beans and lentils in jars or cannisters.

Quick-freezing food on a cooky sheet will prevent foods such as chopped parsley, grated lemon peel, chopped onions, or bell peppers, from sticking together. Put the sheet, with whatever you're going to freeze, directly in the freezer, let it freeze, and then package the food. This allows you to pour a precise amount from the freezer bag.

For quick-freezing, plan ahead, turn the freezer control to minus 10 degrees 24 hours prior to use. Put the food you plan to quick-freeze in the coldest part of the freezer.

Remember a home freezer has a definite capacity for freezing. For instance, in a 20-cubic foot freezer, you can safely freeze 75 pounds of food, simultaneously without thawing what is already there. In a 10-cubic foot freezer you can freeze approximately 35 pounds at one time.

For fast freezing scatter the new packages throughout the freezer. If you butcher your own meat, freeze only the recommended amounts at one time. If possible have all your packaged meat quick-frozen at a locker plant; call first, though, as there is usually a charge for this service.

Freezing eggs

You can freeze egg whites, egg yolks, or whole eggs. Just be sure to freeze in convenient quantities.

Package eggs in small, moisture-vapor-proof containers, leaving 1-inch head-room for expansion. Label the amount of whole eggs, yolks or whites. To thaw leave in the refrigerator overnight. If you are in a great hurry, stand the container in a pan of warm water.

Egg whites. After separating the eggs, pour the whites in containers and freeze. These can be used exactly as fresh egg whites, including whipping for angel food cakes and meringues.

Egg yolks. These need a stabilizer to prevent them from becoming gummy or thick during freezer storage. For each cup of egg yolks, add 2 teaspoons of white corn syrup or sugar or 1 teaspoon of salt. Stir *gently* without incorporating air, package, and freeze.

Whole eggs. These also need a stabilizer. For eggs used in baking, add 2 teaspoons of white corn syrup or sugar to each cup of eggs. For scrambled eggs or omelets, add ½ teaspoon of salt to each cup of eggs. Stir mixture gently before pouring into freezer containers.

When you label the eggs, be sure to include which stabilizer has been added.

I find no difference between frozen and fresh eggs, but remember that most recipes call for the number rather than the amount of eggs. These equivalents will help you in using frozen eggs: 8 egg whites from large eggs equal 1 cup; 12 egg yolks from large eggs equal 1 cup; 5 large eggs equal 1 cup.

Lemon juice

Each year I trade some of our home grown produce, or some cheeses for lemons to freeze. So many recipes call for small bits of lemon peel, or a small amount of juice that it is a real convenience to have some frozen at all times. Pour pure lemon juice into an ice cube tray and you'll have perfect-sized lemon juice cubes for your recipe. Pick out the ripest lemons let them warm up in the kitchen, and roll them around on the counter to soften which will give you more juice.

I use a lemon reamer to separate all the juice from the heavy pulp and seeds, and then freeze the juice. For clearer lemon juice, re-strain and heat to 190 degrees. Chill and freeze. This pasteurization prevents separation when thawing.

Tenderizing poultry

You can tenderize and prepare your own fancy turkey or large roasting chicken by injecting self-basting ingredients. Tenderize them before freezing, or if you buy them frozen, let thaw and tenderize before roasting. A 20cc. syringe, with a number 12 needle (about 3-inches long), can be purchased from a kitchen supply shop for making the injections.

Mix together ½ cup water, ½ cup lemon juice, ½ tablespoon soluble garlic juice, ½ teaspoon Tabasco sauce, and 1 tablespoon salt. Heat to lukewarm and inject up to 200ccs. in various places until the skin swells and tightens. The injected juices tenderize the bird as it cooks by automatically basting it from the inside out. You may wish to brush on butter as the bird roasts.

Freezer jams

Freezer jams cannot be stored on the pantry shelf; they must be frozen and taken out one at a time and stored in the refrigerator while being used. They contain more sugar but have a fresher flavor and color, and are generally superior to cooked jams. Freezer jams do not freeze quite solid with ice crystals and soften quickly for use. Follow the directions included in the package of powdered pectin, and store in half pint jars so you can use a fresh one often.

Fresh frozen strawberry jam

This is almost too good to be jam and is more like a fancy ice cream topping.

2 cups strawberry purée
4 cups sugar
1 package powdered pectin
1 cup water

1. Combine strawberry purée and sugar, let stand 20 minutes, stirring occasionally.

2. Boil pectin in water for one minute, stirring constantly.

3. Add the berries and sugar, stir for 2 minutes off the heat.

4. Pour into containers and let stand for one hour.

5. Refrigerate until cool then store in the freezer. Makes 5 to 6 half pints.

Eggs, when properly frozen, can be used exactly like fresh eggs. Following the directions for whole eggs, beat one egg at a time and pour into individual sections of an ice cube tray. Freeze and package frozen egg cubes in a plastic bag for quick use.

If you're beginning to wonder whether the freezer is infallible, here are a few items it handles imperfectly.

✓Cooked egg whites become rubbery.

✓Mayonnaise separates when thawed.

✓Custard pie is apt to curdle when thawed and meringues on lemon or cream pies shrink and "weep" when frozen.

✓Some cookies with egg whites, crumbly cookies, and some tortes tend to break in storage.

✓When freezing cakes, use a butter-cream frosting. Penuche-type frostings may crack or crumble during freezing, and boiled or seven-minute frostings "weep" when thawed.

The meat department

Having a quantity of meat in the freezer is a great convenience for the cook of the house. There is some controversy, though, whether it is better to buy a whole carcass for the freezer, or just the cuts you use most often.

If your family enjoys the "innards," stews, and will use up every bit of a whole beef, a carcass is indeed economical. For most families it is more economical to buy just the cuts that are used most often; these are the ones to buy on sale. You might for instance, see chuck roast at a good price. Buy one roast, try it immediately, and if you like the quality, buy several more.

Meat storage depends largely on the temperature of the freezer, and the wrapping. Be sure your freezer

maintains a setting of zero degrees or lower.

Freeze hamburger patties, measured hamburger for meat loaf, or one-pound portions for casseroles. You get more mileage out of meats that are proportioned carefully. Try green pepper, onion, and herb seasoning in some of your hamburger patties. The patties can be separated by squares of freezer wrap, or frozen individually on a cookie sheet and then packaged. If the patties are thin, they can be cooked while still frozen. A few individually wrapped chops and small steaks are good to have on hand if your family sometimes eats in shifts.

Buy chickens at a sale price, cut them up, and package. You can currently save about 10 cents a pound if you cut the chicken yourself. Bone chicken breasts and freeze individually for special dishes. I pack the legs and wings together for a fried chicken meal. The backs and necks are so bulky, I freeze them separately, and use for chicken stock later. The giblets can go for another meal; the livers make a great omelet or they can be saved to make paté.

Homemade sausage

With homemade sausage, you'll know exactly what is going in the pot and can season to your own taste.

If you enjoy making your own sausage, you might want to buy a meat-grinder and a sausage-stuffer. The meat market carries cleaned and ready-to-use natural casings. For use soak in warm water to remove most of the salt. There are yards of casing to

an ounce, so don't buy too large a package.

Prior to stuffing, grease the sausage stuffer and attach it to the grinder. Then run the hollow casing over the sausage stuffer. Follow the directions for your grinder. You may need a helper for the stuffing operation, since it is difficult to pack the meat inside the grinder and hold and form the sausages at the same time. Feed the meat into the grinder while it fills the casing. Tie the sausage when it becomes the right size.

Mexican sausage-chorizo

2 pounds ground lean pork or beef
1 clove garlic, mashed
¼ cup mild red wine vinegar
1½ teaspoons salt
2 tablespoons chili powder
1 tablespoon paprika
2 teaspoons oregano
½ teaspoon ground cumin

1. Combine ingredients in a bowl using your hands to work the mixture thoroughly and until the seasonings are completely assimilated.

2. Cover tightly and let age two days in the refrigerator to blend the seasonings.

3. Use for bulk or stuffed sausages.

To make an excellent Mexican bean recipe, add 1 pound fried crumbled chorizo to cooked pinto beans.

Potato sausage

When you have mastered sausage casings, try this recipe.

Sausage casing
1½ pounds lean boneless beef
1 pound lean boneless pork
6 potatoes
1 medium onion, chopped
1 tablespoon salt
¼ teaspoon pepper
1 teaspoon ground allspice

1. Rinse casing and soak in warm water for two hours or overnight.

2. Trim all fat from beef and pork; grind meat together, using the coarse blade of your food chopper.

3. Peel and chop potatoes; you should have exactly 6 cups.

4. Mix together the ground meats, potatoes, onion, salt, pepper, and allspice.

5. Attach the coarse grinder with the sausage stuffer, following instructions for your grinder. Push casing onto the greased stuffer, allowing some to extend beyond the end of the attachment.

6. Grind the meat and potato mixture together letting it run into the casing. Fill the casing firmly, but do not overfill.

Maximum meat storage time

Meat	Refrigerator (36° to 40° F.)	Freezer (at 0°F. or lower)
Beef (fresh)	2 to 4 days	6 to 12 months
Veal (fresh)	2 to 4 days	6 to 9 months
Pork (fresh)	2 to 4 days	3 to 6 months
Lamb (fresh)	2 to 4 days	6 to 9 months
Ground beef, veal and lamb	1 to 2 days	3 to 4 months
Ground pork	1 to 2 days	1 to 3 months
Variety meats	1 to 2 days	3 to 4 months
Luncheon meats	1 week	not recommended
Sausage, fresh pork	1 week	60 days
Sausage, smoked	3 to 7 days	
Sausage, dry and semi-dry (unsliced)	2 to 3 weeks	
Frankfurters	4 to 5 days	1 month
Bacon	5 to 7 days	1 month
Smoked ham, whole	1 week	60 days
Ham slices	3 to 4 days	60 days
Beef, corned	1 week	2 weeks
Leftover cooked meat	4 to 5 days	2 to 3 months

7. Cut off a link 18 inches long, bring the two ends together and tie into a ring. Makes 5 pounds of sausage.

You can make this into smaller sausage links if you wish to freeze it in small units. To cook the thawed sausage, prick the casing with a sterilized needle to allow the fat to escape. Place sausage in a saucepan, cover with water, and simmer 30 to 40 minutes. Don't cook the sausage frozen. It has a tendency to burst.

If you enjoy making sausage, a meat grinder with a sausage stuffing attachment is indispensible. A small smoker gives the homemade sausage a delicious flavor.

Soup packages and reduced stocks

A great way to save time is to make large quantities of soup, and then reduce the bulk and store in the freezer. Soups with reduced water content take up less room in storage and are much easier to thaw and reheat with water and vegetable purées.

Boil all the bones you can accumulate with meat and vegetable trimmings or freeze until there is enough to cook at one time. Crack the bones with a meat saw or cleaver. If possible have the person in your meat department do the hard work. Make a meat stock from several kinds of meat, trimming as much fat as possible. Beef, pork, and fowl make a good mixture. Mix the meats, bones, vegetable pieces and juices, herbs, and ½ cup of red or white wine in a large kettle.

Cover with water and simmer, using less water than called for in your favorite recipe, and you won't have to reduce it as much for storing. The new electric crock pots are excellent for simmering the stock.

When the stock is ready, discard the bones and wilted vegetables. Return the little pieces of meat, add the nicer vegetables you left out of the stock, and finish cooking. If you plan to freeze the soup, chill it quickly. Lift off any fat which has solidified on the top, package, and freeze. Remember you can freeze both the stock and the entire soup.

Black bean soup

1 pound dried black beans, cleaned
3 slices bacon, diced
1 onion, finely chopped
3 cloves garlic, minced
½ pound ham bone and meat
3 small bay leaves
Salt and pepper

1. Place beans in a large soup kettle, cover with water, and bring to a boil. Cook 2 minutes, cover, and let stand for 2 hours (or soak beans in cold water overnight).

2. In a separate pan, cook bacon until half done. Add onion and garlic and sauté until onion is limp.

3. Add onion mixture to beans along with the ham bone and bay leaves and add enough water to cover beans one inch.

4. Cover and cook slowly until beans are tender, about 2 hours.

5. Remove bay leaves, ham bone and meat. When cool enough to handle, tear the meat in small pieces and return to the soup. Season with salt and pepper to taste.

Chill the concentrated soup base, package, and freeze. When you want to use this soup, thin each batch with water or beef stock and be sure to taste for additional seasoning. Serve soup with sliced lemon and a dab of sour cream, if you like.

Minestrone

I keep a bag of pre-soaked beans in the freezer for Minestrone. Soak a quantity of dried beans overnight in cold water. The next day, drain, dry on paper toweling, and freeze in a single layer in large baking pans. When they are frozen, scoop the beans from the pans, package, and return to the freezer. They are handy for baked beans too.

1 onion, finely chopped
⅓ cup diced salt pork
4 tablespoons butter or margarine
¼ cup olive oil
1 carrot, diced
½ cup sliced zucchini
½ small head cabbage, shredded
3 quarts beef stock
1 cup pre-soaked kidney beans
1 cup uncooked rice
2 potatoes, peeled and diced
2 cups canned tomatoes
2 tablespoons chopped parsley
1 clove garlic, minced
¼ teaspoon powdered thyme
¾ cup coarsely chopped Swiss chard
or spinach

1. In a large kettle sauté onion and salt pork in the butter and olive oil until onion is golden but not brown.

2. Add carrot, zucchini, and cabbage; stir and cook 5 minutes.

3. Pour in beef stock and beans; cover and simmer for 2 hours.

4. Add rice, potatoes, and tomatoes if you like them in your Minestrone. Stirring frequently, cook for 30 minutes.

5. Season with parsley, garlic, and thyme; add Swiss chard if you wish.

If mixture is too thick, add more water. Continue simmering for 30 minutes. Season with salt and pepper to taste. Serve with grated Parmesan cheese. Makes 5 quarts.

With garden produce available at any time of the year, soup can be offered year round. Wintertime cabbages, leeks, potatoes in a milk base, and springtime peas are some of the garden produce that enhance soup.

Homemade soup and crackers, both prepared ahead and stored in the freezer, are perfect for a winter lunch.

Crackers

No soup section is complete without cracker recipes. Give variety to crackers with poppy or sesame seed. Both are so inexpensive when purchased in one-quarter pound bags. If well-packaged, crackers can be frozen.

Whole wheat cheese crackers

1 cup (¼ pound) sharp Cheddar cheese, grated
⅓ cup butter
1 cup whole wheat pastry flour
⅛ teaspoon cayenne
¼ teaspoon salt

1. Blend ingredients and shape into a roll 1¼ inches in diameter.

2. Chill or freeze in an airtight can until needed.

3. Slice into ⅛ inch slices and bake on an ungreased baking sheet for 8 to 10 minutes in a 375 degree oven. (Makes about 4 dozen)

Whole wheat crackers

2 cups whole wheat flour
2 teaspoons salt
2 teaspoons baking powder
2 teaspoons brown sugar
½ cup (¼ pound) butter or margarine
⅓ cup milk

1. Sift flour, salt, and baking powder into a bowl.

2. Add brown sugar and butter and cut into flour with a pastry blender or two knives, cutting crosswise, until mixture is fine.

3. Add milk gradually; toss with fork to moisten evenly. Add a few drops more milk if mixture seems dry; it should not stick to the bowl or your hands.

4. Divide dough in four pieces and press each into a ball and flatten

slightly. Place each cake of dough between two pieces of waxed paper and roll out with rolling pin to about 3/16 inch thickness.

5. Peel off top piece of waxed paper, flip dough over onto ungreased cooky sheet, and peel off top piece of paper. Cut into squares or any shape you like. A pizza cutter does a neat job.

6. Prick all over with a fork, then bake in a 375 degree oven 3 to 4 minutes or until lightly browned. Crackers brown quickly so watch them closely.

For variation you can sprinkle poppy, caraway, or sesame seeds over the dough as you roll it out.

Big round crackers

2 cups all-purpose flour *or*
1 cup all-purpose flour and 1 cup rye flour, whole wheat flour, or cornmeal.
2 tablespoons sugar
½ teaspoon salt
½ teaspoon soda
¼ cup (4 tablespoons) shortening
1 cup buttermilk (approximately)

1. Sift together flour, sugar, salt, and soda.

2. Cut in shortening with a pastry blender until mixture is crumbly.

3. Add buttermilk gradually over the top of the mixture tossing with a fork to moisten evenly. Use just enough buttermilk to hold mixture together. The amount will vary slightly with the combination of flours you use.

4. Press into a ball.

5. Pinch off pieces of dough the size of walnuts and roll out on a floured surface to 3/16 inch thickness, turning and flouring to prevent sticking.

6. Place circles of dough on an ungreased baking sheet and prick in several places with a fork.

7. Bake in a 400° oven for 3 to 4 minutes or until golden brown.

Planned-overs

Leftovers are sometimes wasted; *planned-overs* can be calculated successes. For every meal you serve, plan for the next meal. Three baking potatoes in the oven are a lonely sight: next to the potatoes I'd cook an apple cake or a whole winter squash cut in 2 pieces to freeze for a later meal.

Never make a single recipe of the more complicated dishes. Enchiladas, for example, make a thorough mess of the kitchen. Invariably you'll use a little pan for this, a greasy skillet for that, and garnish bowls here and there. Double or quadruple the recipe and freeze. Keep the inventory of these prepared foods up to date, and use them within their "shelf-life" date. Casseroles tend to have a short-freezer-life span, so keep them moving, or your work is wasted.

There is a place in your freezer for special dishes. Check your recipe files to see which of your favorite recipes would be good candidates. Check the freezer cabinet at your market for other frozen entrée possibilities you can duplicate at home.

Special recipes for freezing

Most of these recipes are large enough so that part of the dish can be eaten immediately and the rest frozen for later use.

Polynesian chicken

This is a very large recipe and will provide you with several casseroles to freeze.

2 cans (No. 2 *each*) pineapple chunks
2 cups diced green pepper
6 cups diagonally sliced celery
1 cup chicken broth
¼ cup cornstarch
¼ cup sugar
¼ cup vinegar
2 tablespoons soy sauce
3 tablespoons butter or margarine
1 can (3 oz.) sliced mushrooms, drained
1 flat can (6 oz.) water chestnuts, drained and sliced
3 cups diced cooked chicken
1 cup cashew nuts

1. Drain liquid from pineapple and reserve.

2. Simmer green pepper in ⅔ cup of the pineapple syrup for 10 minutes.

3. Simmer celery in chicken broth until it looks transparent (about 10 minutes).

4. In a saucepan, combine cornstarch, sugar, vinegar, and soy sauce until smooth. Add the liquids from

the green pepper and celery and stirring, cook until thick and clear.

5. Sauté drained pineapple chunks in butter for 3 minutes. Combine green pepper, celery, sauce, pineapple chunks, mushrooms, water chestnuts, and chicken; stir lightly.

6. Spoon into several small containers and freeze.

To serve, thaw the desired amount, heat in 400 degree oven, stir in cashew nuts, and serve over crisp Chinese noodles or rice. Do not freeze the cashews in the sauce, as they tend to soften. Makes about 15 one-cup servings.

Mariel's enchiladas

Dipping tortillas in hot water instead of frying them helps keep the cholesterol and calorie count down and the dishwasher one frying pan closer to completion.

- **1 large onion, finely chopped**
- **2 cloves garlic, minced**
- **1 green pepper, seeded and chopped**
- **3 tablespoons olive oil**
- **4 tablespoons flour**
- **2 tablespoons chili powder**
- **2 cans (6 oz. *each*) tomato paste**
- **2 cups beef stock or 2 bouillon cubes dissolved in 2 cups hot water**
  Salt
- **1¼ pounds ground round**
- **1 dozen corn or flour tortillas**
  Green onions, ripe olives, and Cheddar cheese for garnish

1. Sauté onion, garlic, and green pepper in olive oil until vegetables are limp.

2. Sprinkle flour and chili powder into onion mixture and stir until blended.

3. Combine tomato paste and beef stock and pour into the onion mixture. Cook until smooth and thickened, stirring frequently. Add salt to taste.

4. In a separate pan, cook ground round and one-fourth of the cooked sauce until meat is browned and crumbly.

5. Dip one tortilla in hot water for 5 seconds and drain.

6. Spoon about 3 tablespoons meat filling down the center of tortilla. Roll tortilla around filling and place, flap side down, in a greased shallow casserole. Place filled enchiladas side by side.

7. Spoon the remaining three-fourths cooked sauce over the surface of the casserole.

8. Cool Enchiladas, cover, and freeze.

To use, bake, uncovered, while still frozen, in a 375 degree oven for 30 to 40 minutes or until hot and bubbly. Scatter chopped green onions, chopped ripe olives, and grated Cheddar cheese over Enchiladas before serving. Serves 6.

Annie's Subzi

The exotic name for squash Pakistani style is Subzi. Preparation is easier than pronunciation. I like to freeze a dozen or more packages when summer squash is abundant.

- **1 onion, cut in half, then thinly sliced**
- **4 tablespoons (½ cube) butter or margarine**
- **½ teaspoon cumin seed**
- **1 teaspoon *each* salt, garlic powder, and curry powder**
- **½ teaspoon *each* ground cumin, allspice, ginger, and chili powder**
- **¼ teaspoon *each* turmeric, cayenne, and ground cardamom**
- **1 tomato, peeled and chopped**
- **6 summer squash, zucchini, crookneck, or scalloped**
- **¼ cup water**

1. Sauté onion in butter with cumin seed until onion is limp and clear.

2. In a small cup mix salt, garlic powder, curry powder, ground cumin, allspice, ginger, chili powder, turmeric, cayenne, and cardamom. Sprinkle over the onion and cook until it thickens.

3. Add tomato and simmer until the liquid is reduced.

4. Add squash and stir-fry 5 minutes.

5. Add water and simmer until squash is tender and mixture is quite thick.

Many Mexican dishes can be prepared in advance and frozen, using a variety of homemade foods including, cheese, salsa, homemade tortillas, and dried and pickled peppers.

Pie crusts and fillings can be frozen separately ahead of time for quick assembly when you don't have the time to start from scratch.

Apricot toaster tarts

Try homemade pop-up tarts as an interesting breakfast idea. You can make them any time you have purée in the freezer.

Filling:
 1 cup apricot thick purée
⅓ cup sugar
¼ teaspoon cinnamon
¼ cup chopped walnuts

1. Blend all ingredients together.

2. Prepare your favorite pastry using 2 cups flour and add milk in place of the water. Divide dough in half and roll each half into a 9 x 16 inch rectangle. Cut each rectangle into 12 pieces 3 inches by 4 inches.

3. Place a spoonful of apricot filling on 12 of the pieces.

4. Dampen the edges of the remaining 12 pieces and place carefully on the filled halves.

5. Press a fork around the edges to make sure you have an extra tight seal.

6. Lightly bake on an ungreased baking sheet in a 400 degree oven for 10 to 12 minutes or until set. They should brown later when toasted.

7. After cooling, wrap individually and freeze. Toast them at the lightest setting. Don't hesitate to try other fruit fillings.

Mariel's cheesecake

Try freezing freshmade cheese-cake without wrapping; this won't mar the soft surface. Then cut into neat wedges, wrap, and store.

¼ cup melted butter or margarine
 4 double graham crackers, crushed
 2 pounds dry cottage cheese
 3 tablespoons flour
   Dash of salt
 1 cup sugar
 1 teaspoon pure vanilla
   Juice of 1 lemon
 4 eggs
 1 cup sour cream

1. Brush melted butter on sides and bottom of a 9-inch spring form pan.

2. Sprinkle three-fourths of the graham cracker crumbs in the pan and shake to coat bottom and sides.

3. Sieve cottage cheese; mix with flour, salt, sugar, vanilla, and lemon juice.

4. Beat in eggs one at a time.

5. Fold in sour cream.

6. Spoon into crumb-lined pan, then top with remaining graham cracker crumbs.

7. Bake in 325 degree oven for 1 hour and 15 minutes or until a knife inserted in the center comes out clean.

Leave until quite cold in the cooling oven so it won't fall.

8. Chill and then freeze.

Marge's bar cookies

These are a cake-type bar cooky— a freezer favorite for lunch boxes.

 2 cups raisins
 2 cups water
 1 cup shortening
 2 cups sugar
3½ cups all-purpose flour
1½ teaspoons *each* salt and soda
 1 teaspoon *each* ground cloves, cinnamon, and nutmeg
 2 eggs

1. Boil raisins in water for 2 minutes.

2. Remove from heat, add shortening and sugar, stir until blended, and cool.

3. Sift flour with salt, soda, cloves, cinnamon, and nutmeg into raisin mixture and stir until well mixed.

4. Beat eggs and add.

5. Pour into two greased 9- by 13-inch baking pans. Bake in a 375 degree oven for 20 minutes. Remove from oven and while still hot, glaze with frosting.

Frosting. Mix ½ pound powdered sugar with 1 tablespoon melted butter, 4 drops lemon extract, and enough hot water to facilitate spreading (about 1 tablespoon). Spread over hot cookies. When cool, cut into generous squares, and freeze.

Freezer cookies

A very large cookie recipe just for the freezer (for 312 cookies).

2 cups brown sugar, firmly packed
2 cups granulated sugar
3 cups (1½ pounds) butter or margarine
6 eggs
1½ teaspoons hot water
1 tablespoon vanilla
1 tablespoon salt
6¾ cups all-purpose flour
3 large packages (12 oz. *each*) chocolate chips
2½ cups chopped walnuts

1. Cream brown sugar, granulated sugar, and butter until smooth.

2. Beat in eggs, one at a time.

3. Stir in water, vanilla, and salt.

4. Add flour and mix until well blended, using your hands if necessary.

5. Work chocolate chips and nuts into the dough.

6. Drop dough by a small spoonful onto greased cooky sheets. Bake in a 375 degree oven for 10 minutes or until lightly browned.

If possible, bake on two cookie sheets at a time and have two more sheets ready to go when the first two are done. Cool cookies on racks, package, and freeze. There you have it, 26 dozen cookies.

Lunchbox ideas

With a home freezer you can avoid the problem of assembling a sack lunch minutes before the school bus arrives. Every September I plan to do better at keeping sandwiches in the freezer for lunchboxes or for weekend meals when we have an outside project going on.

For a well-stocked lunch freezer, turn on the music, bring out the breads, spreads and fillings, and have a sandwich marathon.

Sometimes I purposely cook a large turkey or ham so there will be lots of meat for fillings. Make a batch of mustard or horseradish flavored butter for the ham sandwiches, anchovy or herb flavored butter for the turkey (see page 58). Use a variety of breads such as whole wheat, rye, French rolls, or bagels. Spread both halves of the bread with butter. It not only adds flavor but insulates the bread during freezing and thawing and prevents sogginess. Top with sliced meat. Add sliced pickle and cheese or not, as you wish. Package in individual plastic sandwich bags, then put each variety in a large plastic bag, label, and freeze. When you pack the lunch add a little bag of lettuce or sprouts. The thawing frozen

Suitability of vegetables for freezing

Vegetable	Suitability for freezing	Comments
Asparagus	excellent	
Beans, green	good	Tendercrop and closely related varieties and Blue Lake varieties either bush or pole are preferred because of their good flavor. Also, Blue Lake has a desirable thick flesh.
Beans, wax	good	
Lima Beans, green	excellent	Fordhook types preferred.
Beets	fair	Better canned; select small roots only for freezing.
Broccoli	excellent	
Cabbage	not recommended	Preserve as sauerkraut.
Carrots	fair	Select tender roots only. Can be diced and frozen with peas.
Cauliflower	excellent	Also suitable for pickling.
Celery	not recommended	Except in "soup packages."
Chinese Cabbage	not recommended	Use in sauerkraut.
Cucumbers	not recommended	Preserve by pickling (see notes below).
Eggplant	fair	Significant quality loss; suitable for casserole dishes.
Kale	good	Select young leaves only.
Kohlrabi	fair	Significant quality loss, picks up *high* flavor.
Lettuce	not recommended	
Muskmelon	fair	Firm fleshed varieties are preferred; freeze small pieces; use within 3 months.
Mustard	good	Select tender leaves and remove stems.
Onions	fair	Freeze chopped, mature onions; significant quality loss; use in 3 months.
Parsley	not recommended	Can be dried.
Parsnips	fair	Significant quality loss.
Peas	excellent	Frosty and Perfected Freezer 60 preferred. All large wrinkled seeded varieties are suitable and so are edible podded varieties.
Peppers	fair	Significant quality loss; better if frozen chopped; use in 3 months.
Potatoes	not recommended	Store fresh at 40-50° F.
Pumpkins	not recommended	
Radishes	not recommended	
Rhubarb	excellent	Varieties with red stalks like Canada Red, Valentine, and Ruby preferred. Pull stalks soon after they reach full size.
Swiss Chard	good	Select only tender leaves; remove midrib or stems.
Spinach	excellent	Savoy varieties are often preferred.
Summer squash	fair	Significant quality loss.
Winter squash	good	Be sure squash is fully mature (hard rind); freeze cooked pieces or mash.
Sweet corn	good to excellent	Jubilee, Seneca Chief, Golden Cross, and Silver Queen preferred; corn on cob frozen without blanching should be eaten in 6-8 weeks.
Tomatoes	fair	Better canned; freeze only juice or cooked tomatoes.
Turnips & Rutabagas	fair	Significant quality loss.
Watermelon	fair	Freeze only as pieces; use within 3 months.

Notes:
The term "significant quality loss" means the product after being frozen is quite inferior to the fresh product.

For cucumber pickles, use pickling varieties if many pickles are to be made, though young slicing cucumbers are suitable for quick-method dills.

In canning, the variety is seldom of major consideration for quality in home canning. Vegetables harvested at peak of quality and processed promptly usually will provide a high quality product regardless of variety. Tomato varieties should be chosen with the family preferences for mild or acid flavors in mind. Chart by Ruth Klippstein and P. A. Minges, Home Garden Dept. of Vegetable Crops, Cornell University.

sandwich will keep the lunch box cool, even in warm weather.

Usually I make a few sandwiches at a time from "planned over" meats, such as a roast, meat loaf, corned beef, or tongue. With a variety of breads from the freezer, it takes only a few minutes to put these together right after dinner; it also keeps the food from disappearing during a late evening raid on the refrigerator.

Ground cooked meat and chopped chicken are good for meat or chicken salad sandwiches, and freeze well if mixed with salad dressing. When I want to use mayonnaise as a binder I freeze little tubs of the ground meat. I thaw it in the refrigerator the night before I want to use it, add the mayonnaise in the morning along with diced celery. I've found that quantities of mayonnaise will separate when thawing, therefore it's better to add it just before using.

You can also plan ahead and freeze "hot" sandwiches. Mix equal parts of ground ham, canned luncheon meat, or corned beef and ground processed cheese. Season with a little mustard and catsup. Stuff hot dog buns with this filling, wrap individually in aluminum foil, and freeze. Reheat frozen rolls, still wrapped in foil, in a 350 degree oven for 25 minutes. Flaked tuna or salmon, a little sautéed diced celery, and grated cheese are other good fillings for hot sandwiches. The cheese melts to a creamy consistency and binds the filling together.

Ice cream and sherbet

A chapter on freezing wouldn't be complete without recipes for ice cream and sherbet; here are a few of my favorites.

Strawberry 4-H sherbet

Purée 4 boxes of washed and stemmed strawberries. Mix with 4 cups sugar, ¼ cup lemon juice, and 1 quart buttermilk. Freeze, using a hand freezer.

If you have any left over, freeze in a wide-mouth mason jar and serve on a slice of angel food cake.

Fresh apricot ice cream

Dip 2 pounds fresh apricots (a few at a time) in hot water for 30 seconds or until the skins slip off easily when peeled. Cut in half, remove pits, and purée in blender or food mill. Combine the purée with 1¼ cups sugar, 2 cups half and half, 2 cups whipping cream, 1 cup milk, a dash of salt, and 1 teaspoon vanilla. Pour into a hand-freezer container and freeze using a mixture of 1 cup salt to 3 quarts crushed ice.

Fresh apricot sherbet

Purée 1 pound of freshly peeled apricots. Mix with ¾ cup sugar, 1½ cups milk, and 1 teaspoon vanilla. Fold in 2 egg whites beaten stiff. Pour into freezer tray and freeze until slushy, about 2 hours. Transfer to chilled mixer bowl and beat to break up ice crystals. Return to the freezer tray and freeze overnight. Makes one quart, which is never enough for a real apricot sherbet lover.

Lemon sherbet

Boil 4 cups water and 2 cups sugar together for 3 minutes; cool, then add 1 cup lemon juice, 1 teaspoon grated lemon peel, and a dash of salt. Fold in 3 egg whites beaten stiff. Pour into freezer tray and freeze until slushy. Transfer to chilled mixer bowl and beat to break up ice crystals. Return to the freezer tray and freeze overnight. Makes 1 quart.

Frozen popsicles

By making and storing your own popsicles, you'll always have something when someone asks, "What's there to eat?" I buy 1000 meat skewers at the meat counter for less than one dollar. The sticks are also handy for forming meat in skirt steak rolls, making taffy apples, and skewered beef.

Sweeten any fruit purée, thin down, and mold in small paper cups or regular popsicle molds. Add the sticks when partly frozen. Try orange, grape, strawberry, and other juices, as well as thinned purées. It doesn't take long to have young volunteers for this job.

Frozen purées and juices

Fruit purées and juices can be made from overripe and frozen fruit. Crushed and sugared fruit is perfectly delicious in jam, ice cream, sherbets, and even puddings. Clean, sort, and crush very ripe fruit in a blender or a food mill. Soft berries need only be mashed.

If the fruit is not as soft as you'd like, steam a bit in water and then purée. Use 1 cup sugar to 6 to 8 cups purée. Sometimes I add ascorbic acid to keep pale colored fruit such as bananas from turning black. Freeze in measured amounts for your favorite recipes. Puréed fruits in measured amounts can be used later for jams. Pack the puréed fruit earmarked for jam in heavy plastic bags. I usually don't even consider making jam until after Christmas.

Pure unsugared juices should be saved for use in clear jellies. Make a purée, but drain the juice through

a jelly bag. Do not disturb or try to help force the juice. The juice should be remarkably clear. I have noticed that frozen jelly juice will often have a little sediment on the bottom of the frozen block when removed from the freezer. Remove with a sharp knife before it has a chance to thaw.

Few desserts can compare to homemade ice cream and sherbet, especially with the addition of fresh fruit.

Ways to freeze

VEGETABLE	SELECTION	PREPARATION	BLANCHING	PACKING
Artichokes	Small whole, or heart	Cut off top of bud and trim to cone; wash	Boiling: 8 minutes Steaming: 8-10 minutes	Cool, pack and freeze
Asparagus	Young green stalks	Rinse and sort for size. Cut in convenient lengths to fit container	2-4 minutes	Cool, pack and freeze
Beans, green	Pick desired lengths	Wash and drain; snip ends and cut as desired	3-4 minutes	Cool, pack and freeze
Beans, lima	Slightly rounded, bright green pods	Wash	4 minutes	Drain and shell; rinse in cold water. Pack and freeze
Beans, shelled	Well-filled, bright green, tender pods	Wash	Boiling: 2 minutes Steaming: 3 minutes	Cool, pack and freeze
Beets	Tender and mild flavored	Wash, leave ½ inch of top	Cook whole until tender	Skin and cut, if desired. Cool, pack and freeze
Broccoli	Well formed heads	Rinse, peel and trim; split lengthwise into pieces not more than ½ inch across	Boiling: 3 minutes Steaming: 5 minutes	Cool, pack and freeze
Brussels sprouts	Green buds	Rinse and trim; remove outer leaves	3-5 minutes	Cool, pack and freeze
Cabbage	Firm, fresh, no discolored leaves	Trim outer leaves; shred or cut into wedges	Shredded: Boiling: 1½ minutes Steaming: 3 minutes Wedges: Boiling: 3 minutes Steaming: 4 minutes	Cool, pack and freeze
Carrots	Tender, mild flavored	Trim, wash and peel. Small carrots can be left whole. Cut others into ¼ inch slices	Boiling: 2-5 minutes Steaming: 4-5 minutes	Cool, pack and freeze
Cauliflower	Solid, well formed, snow-white heads	Break or cut into flowerets	Boiling: 3 minutes Steaming: 4 minutes	Cool, pack and freeze
Celery	Crisp stalks	Clean well. Cut across rib into 1-inch pieces	Boiling: 3 minutes Steaming: 4 minutes	Cool, pack and freeze. (Does not freeze well; good only for use in soups, stews and casseroles.)
Corn whole kernel	Young, tender kernels	Husk ears, remove silk; and trim ends	Scald in boiling water 4½ minutes. Keep kettle covered	Cool in ice water, drain. Cut kernels from cobs at about ¾ depth of kernels
Corn on-the-cob	Small ears up to 1½ inches diameter	Husk ears, remove silk; trim ends	Scald in boiling water 8 minutes	Chill quickly in ice water, drain, pack and freeze
Eggplant	Firm, heavy and of uniform good color	Wash, peel and cut into ½-inch slices or cubes. Dip in solution of 1 tablespoon lemon juice to 1 quart water	4 minutes	Dip again in lemon juice solution after heating and cooling. Pack and freeze

VEGETABLE	SELECTION	PREPARATION	BLANCHING	PACKING
Greens (Kale, collards, turnips, spinach, etc.)	Small and tender	Rinse well. Trim leaves from stems	2-3 minutes (Stir to prevent matting)	Cool, pack and freeze
Kohlrabi	Tender and mild flavor	Trim off trunk and wash; slice into small pieces	1-2 minutes	Cool, pack and freeze
Mushrooms	Firm, tender, small to medium	Wash and trim stems; leave whole or slice	Add ⅓ teaspoon lemon juice to 1 gallon water Boiling: 2-4 minutes Steaming: 3-5 minutes	Cool, pack and freeze
Okra	Young, tender pods	Wash and cut off tip end of stems	Boiling: 2-3 minutes Steaming: 5 minutes	Cool, freeze whole or slice crosswise
Parsnips	Smooth roots	Remove tips; wash and peel; slice and cube	3 minutes	Cool, pack and freeze
Peas	Plump and rounded pods. Freeze day of harvest	Shell, do not wash	1½ minutes	Cool, pack and freeze
Peppers	Fully ripe	Wash and halve; remove seeds and pulp; slice or dice	2 minutes, if desired	Cool, pack and freeze
Soybeans	Well rounded, green pods	Wash	5 minutes	Cool and shell; rinse in cold water; pack and freeze
Spinach	Young, tender leaves	Wash thoroughly to remove grit	Boiling: 3 minutes	Cool, pack and freeze
Squash	Pumpkin and winter squash fully colored and hard shelled. Summer squash before rind is hard	Wash, pare and cut into small pieces	Winter: Cook completely, without seasoning Summer: 4 minutes Zucchini: 2-3 minutes	Cool, pack and freeze
Sweet potatoes	Smooth, firm	Wash	Cook in water or bake at 350° F. until soft	Cool and remove skins if desired. Cool, pack and freeze
Swiss Chard	Young tender leaves	Wash thoroughly to remove grit	Boiling: 3 minutes	Cool, pack and freeze
Tomatoes, whole	Firm, ripe	Wash and dry		Pack and freeze. (Use within one month.)
Tomatoes, stewed	Firm, ripe	Wash and quarter	Simmer without water in heavy pot for 20 minutes. Stir continuously	Chill, pack and freeze
Turnips	Young, tender roots	Cut off tops, wash and peel, slice or cube	2½ minutes	Chill pack and freeze

Drying and smoking

Two of the oldest and most efficient methods for preserving a bounty of fruit, vegetables, herbs, meats, and fish.

Drying is a very simple process requiring only low heat, a good draft, and, in the case of cabinet-drying, shade for retention of color and vitamins. There are a number of ways of drying an item, including sun-drying, cabinet-drying (in some parts of the country called dehydrator drying), sulphur-drying, and smoking and curing.

Sun drying

If conditions are ideal and the produce thinly cut, fruits and vegetables will dry in two to three days. During the drying process stir and sort the pieces to insure an even dry and to prevent any mold development. Both fruits and vegetables will be stiff and leathery when dry. You can also test for dryness by cutting into the produce; if there is any moisture in the center, longer drying is indicated.

The ideal conditions for sun drying are rather limited. The area where you place the drying racks or trays should get a maximum amount of heat and sunlight. If your climate is naturally humid, it is difficult to get a good dry outdoors. Wherever you find a spot the daytime temperature should be 100 degrees or more. These high temperatures can be achieved, even though the air temperature is not that high, by placing the racks where they will receive reflected heat, such as on a roof. The drying trays should be brought indoors at night if there is more than a 20 degree difference between the day and night temperature.

In some areas of the country cool or humid summer weather makes outdoor sun drying an uncertain process. A drying cabinet changes that and allows you to dry fruits, vegetables and other treats without fear of the weather.

Cabinet or dehydrator drying

A home drying cabinet or dehydrator is easy to build. The heat source you use depends on your imagination and some experimentation. Try using a small portable heater or an electric or gas hot plate that can be turned down to 110 degrees or lower.

Any heat source should be considered and tried, but be sure to take careful precautions against overheating and possible fire.

Drying meats in the controlled conditions of a drying cabinet has several distinct advantages. For example, it is difficult to keep a dog or cat away from drying jerky, if you are drying it in the open. Similarly, fruit leather seems to collect all types of interesting bugs if dried outdoors, and it's a

Warm dry weather and a location with maximum sunlight are necessary for drying produce outdoors. Here a gravel driveway proves the right spot.

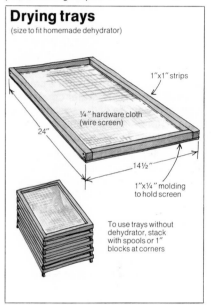

Drying trays
(size to fit homemade dehydrator)

1"x1" strips

¼" hardware cloth (wire screen)

24"

14½"

1"x¼" molding to hold screen

To use trays without dehydrator, stack with spools or 1" blocks at corners

real chore plucking them out of the sticky fruit as it dries. Covering the fruit leather with cheesecloth isn't the complete answer either; a strong gust of wind and the cloth, support and all, will wind up in a sticky mess.

Drying food in a controlled heat source, in a nice clean cabinet, away from bugs, blowing cheesecloth, and cats and dogs, is more appealing to me all the time. Aside from these advantages the drying cabinet can also be used to maintain the proper temperature for rising bread, culturing yogurt, and making homemade sour cream or buttermilk.

Once you have mastered the drying technique you might try some of these more unusual ideas which have worked well for me.

✓ For instant soup, drop mounds of pureé of bean or other thick soups on heavy duty plastic film and dry into little wafers—reconstitute in a cup of boiling water.

◁

Once a necessity for preservation, smoked salmon and other types of fresh fish are now considered a delicacy. Using a sharp knife, cut whole cleaned salmon into manageable chunks. Filet the chunks by slipping the knife just under the rib cage through to the back bone on both sides. Leaving the skin intact cut thru the back of the fish, leaving two individual filets. Filets are placed in a small commercial smoker and processed according to directions on page 59.

Old panty hose makes an innovative onion drier. Knots are tied between onions for use one at a time.

Vegetable ideas

A surprisingly large number of vegetables are sold in their dry state. Dried vegetables are great for soups and a good addition to camping trips.

You can process string beans, beets, carrots, corn, onions, peas, mixed soup vegetables, spinach, potatoes, or any other variety that suits your taste in a home cabinet dryer. Pick or buy the vegetables at their prime, blanch if necessary, and dry immediately.

Corn is a delicious dried product. Try this recipe which I have used successfully for years. Slice two quarts raw corn right off the cob. Do not blanch. Mix with 6 tablespoons sugar, 2 to 4 teaspoons salt, (depending on your taste) and ½ cup cream. Boil gently in a heavy pan for 20 minutes, stirring almost constantly. Remove and spread out in the drying cabinet, stirring from time to time until crispy. Store in jars. To use, reconstitute with milk and cook briefly until tender.

Working with dry beans

Growing dry beans has been a great success for us. We have tried out 8 or 9 different dry bean varieties, and now have settled on a couple that do the best for us in our climate. With careful weight tests, we found the average yield was about 10 pounds dry beans from 1 pound of seeds.

One of our favorite dry bean varieties is the Dwarf Horticultural bean which is also meaty and delicious in the green stage. We eat some green and let the rest dry to maturity. This particular bean matures into a fat, pink and purple spotted bean. It retains its shape and meatiness during cooking.

Dried corn stores well and can be reconstituted with milk for a good side dish.

I pick the beans when they are dry, but still in the pod. I shell a few each day until the whole batch is plucked. I let them dry further in a drying cabinet or in the sun, reducing the moisture even more. This particular bean is excellent in cooking, stays big and round, and doesn't mush up.

Any bean that matures can be dried, such as wax beans, scarlet runner, or limas. When the bean patch seems to grow faster than you can move, simply walk away and let them dry on the vine.

Should the weather turn frosty or damp when you are about to harvest, leave the beans in their pods and dry in a warm airy place. If you shell them while still wet, the beans might mildew.

When the pods are dry, we put them in a big barrel and beat them with a pole, trying to work the beans free from the pods. We put the whole mess on hardware cloth stretched over a frame; the beans usually drop through and the pods stay on top. Some winnowing and sorting will always be necessary even under the best of conditions.

To winnow, drop the beans from a high spot above a container. The wind (if there is no wind, use an electric fan) will separate the chaff from the bean. We found that the livestock crave the dry bean pods. They could hear us beating the pods with the pole and set up an awful bellowing each time we did this job.

After any treatment, store the beans in airtight cans or jars with tight lids in a cool, dry place. Dried beans must be soaked overnight in water to soften for cooking. If you bring the cleaned and sorted beans to a boil for 2 minutes, and then let stand for an hour or two, it shortens the soaking time considerably.

Nut storage

Walnuts and other nuts can be dried after the outside husks are removed. Be sure to wear gloves while husking the nuts; walnut husks will stain your hands, seemingly forever, if you don't take this precaution. A weakened bleach solution will help remove the stains.

Spread the nuts out on trays or a big canvas and dry in the sun. Crack open one or two nuts to check the drying meat. The membrane between the two nut halves should be brittle. Do not attempt to store the nuts in a closed container if they are at all damp. I like to crack the walnuts the minute they are dry enough; if cracked early the nuts will be fresh enough so that almost every one will crack into a perfect half.

Without the protective outer shell, the nuts will turn rancid without refrigeration, freezing, or some type of treatment. Many cookbooks suggest baking or cooking the nuts for further drying. University studies have shown, however, that the higher temperatures tend to break down the oil, making it rancid.

Dried nuts can be stored up to 12 months in the refrigerator and indefinitely in the freezer.

Toasted nuts

Toasting nuts is not necessary for preservation—just for good flavor. To toast spread shelled nuts on a shallow pan and heat in a 300 degree oven for 30 minutes.

For roasted salted nuts spread the nuts in a pan and add 1 teaspoon salad oil, butter, or margarine per cup of nuts. Sprinkle with a light coating of salt, and heat in a 300 degree oven for 30 minutes. Spread the oiled nuts on paper towels to cool.

Salted sunflower seeds

Add sunflower seeds and 2 tablespoons of salt to a large container of hot water. Soak overnight. Drain, rinse the seeds lightly with fresh water, and spread them on toweling to dry. As the seeds soak in the hot water, they swell and absorb the brine. As they dry out, the salt crystalizes inside on the meat of the sunflower seed.

If the seeds aren't salty enough, adjust the next time you try the recipe. Some seeds are more porous than others and will absorb more of the salt. Experiment with the quantity of salt brine. This method also works well with raw peanuts, pumpkin and squash seeds.

56

Drying of fruits

Fruit	Preparation	Treat before drying — Choose one of the following 3 methods.			Test for dryness (cool before testing)
		Sulphur (preferred)	Steam blanch*	Water blanch*	
Apples	Peel and core, cut into slices or rings about ⅛ inch thick.	60 minutes	Steam 5 minutes, depending on texture	—	Soft, pliable, no moist area in center when cut in half
Apricots	Pit and halve for steam blanch or sulphuring. For water blanch, leave whole and pit and halve after blanch.	4-5 hours	Steam, 3-4 minutes	4-5 minutes	Same as apples
Figs	Preferable to partly dry on tree. Normally drop from tree when ⅔ dry. Leave whole.		Syrup blanch (see page 55)		Flesh pliable, slightly sticky but not wet
Grapes	Leave whole. Grapes dry in less time if dipped in lye 10 seconds.**		No treatment necessary.		Raisinlike texture, no moist center
Nectarines and peaches	When sulphuring, pit and halve. If desired, remove skins. If sliced or quartered sulphur 1 hour.	1-2 hours	Steam 5 minutes if halved, 8 minutes if whole. Skin can be removed after blanching.	8 minutes; skin can be removed after blanching	Same as apples
Pears	Cut in half and core. Peeling preferred.	1 hour	Steam 6 minutes (peeled, will be soft)	—	Same as apples
Persimmons	Use firm fruit as ripe is too difficult to handle. Using stainless steel knife, peel, slice.		No treatment necessary.		Light to medium brown, tender but not sticky
Prunes	For sun-drying, dip in boiling lye solution** to check skins.		No treatment necessary.		Leathery; pit should not slip when squeezed

* If you cannot sulphur out of doors you may steam or water blanch. However the fruit is soft and hot to handle. If fruit is not sulphured it will darken. The fruit is safe to use but is not attractive or pleasing in color. Follow directions on page 54 for sulphuring and pages 93-96 for steam or water blanch.

** See page 55 for making lye solution.

Drying vegetables

Variety	Preparation	Advance treatment	How many minutes	Test for dryness
Beans: bush varieties such as Refugee and Stringless Green Pod	Remove defective pods. Wash. Remove strings from string varieties, Split pods lengthwise, to hasten drying.	Steam or Pressure saucepan	15 to 20 / 5	brittle
Beets	Select small, tender beets of good color and flavor, free from woodiness. Wash; trim the tops but leave the crowns; steam for 30 to 45 minutes, until cooked through. Cool; trim off the roots and crowns; peel. Cut into shoestring strips or into slices about ⅛ inch thick.	No further treatment		tough; leathery
Broccoli	Trim and cut as for serving. Wash. Quarter stalks lengthwise.	Steam	8 to 10	brittle
Cabbage	Remove outer leaves, quarter, and core. Cut into shreds about ⅛ inch thick.	Steam	5 to 6 wilt	tough to brittle
Carrots	Select crisp, tender carrots, free from woodiness. Wash. Trim off the roots and tops. Cut into slices or strips about ⅛ inch thick.	Steam	8 to 10	tough; leathery
Corn, cut	Select tender, sweet corn. Husk. Steam on the cob immediately, 10 or 15 minutes, or until milk is set. Cut from cob. Husk.	No further treatment		dry; brittle
Corn, on the cob		Steam	30	dry; brittle
Leaves for seasoning: celery; parsley		Wash		brittle
Onions	Remove outer discolored layers. Slice.	No further treatment		brittle; light-colored
Peas	Select young, tender peas of a sweet variety. Shell.	Steam immediately	10	hard; wrinkled; shatter when hit with a hammer
Potatoes	Peel, cut into shoestring strips 3/16 inch in cross section, or cut into slices about ⅛ inch thick.	Rinse in cold water; steam	4 to 6	brittle
Spinach and other greens	Select young, tender leaves. Wash. See that leaves are not wadded when placed on trays. Cut large leaves crosswise into several pieces to facilitate drying.	Steam	4, or until thoroughly wilted	brittle
Squash (banana)	Wash, peel, and slice in strips ¼ inch thick.	Steam	6	tough to brittle
Squash (Hubbard) Pumpkin, yellow	Chop into strips about 1 inch wide. Peel off the rind. Scrape off the fiber and seeds. Cut peeled strips crosswise into pieces about ⅛ inch thick.	Steam	Until tender	tough to brittle
Squash, summer: crookneck, scallop, zucchini, etc.	Wash, trim, and cut into ¼ -inch slices.	Steam	6	brittle
Tomatoes for stewing	Select tomatoes of good color. Steam or dip in boiling water to loosen skins. Chill in cold water. Peel. Cut into sections, not over ¾ inch wide. Cut small pear or plum tomatoes in half.	No further treatment or may sulfur	10 to 20	leathery

Gathering and drying herbs

The best time to harvest leaves of most herbs for drying is just before the flowers open, early in the morning before the heat of day.

When I walk through the garden and see that various herbs are ready to pick, I wait no longer. I pick a nice bunch right then and fasten a rubber band around the stems and hang them overhead in the kitchen for fast drying. I've found that it takes too much time to harvest any crop in one fell swoop, so I do most things piecemeal this way.

After the bundles are dry, I lay out some newspaper and shred off the perfect leaves and buds onto the paper and discard the heavier stems and branches. It only takes a week for a good dry on most herbs. When dried quickly this way the herbs retain a greener, brighter color.

In bad weather, or when I am forced to work with a lot of drying all at once, I use the dehydrator. While the bundles of herbs are drying, I enjoy their fragrance, and the handiness of having the bunches right in the kitchen where I can snip off pieces to use.

You can cut back most herb plants several times during the summer; they seem to grow better after the trim. With perennial herbs, allow enough time to re-grow before the winter arrives. Harvest the annual herbs before frost is expected.

Large leaved herbs are better dried with the leaves taken off and separated for faster drying. The smaller leaved herbs should be dried while on the stems. After they are crumbly dry, store the leaves in tightly lidded jars or bottles.

Some people claim dark jars are best because they eliminate light and save the color. I store herbs in clear or blue oil-sample bottles, with tight corks where there is no light, and store the larger supply of herbs in tightly lidded coffee cans.

The herb pot

Keep a little covered pot on the counter near your stove. When you pick fresh herbs for cooking, add any leftovers to the pot. The combination will change from day to day, making an interesting blend.

Drying parsley

Try the old-fashioned method for drying parsley by tying them into small bunches with string. Dip briefly into boiling water. Heat the oven to 400 degrees. Add the parsley sprigs, turn off the oven, and dry the parsley in the oven heat.

Herb salt

A nice taste for any meat or casserole dish. Pound the following dried herbs with a mortar and pestle set until blended, ¼ cup parsley flakes, 1 tablespoon basil leaves, 1 tablespoon dried oregano leaves, 1 tablespoon paprika, 1 teaspoon celery leaves, and 1 cup salt. Store in a salt shaker for instant use.

Herb butters

Make herb butters by creaming a quarter pound of soft butter with a tablespoon or so of dried or fresh herbs. Blend well together and serve over meats or vegetables. Try garlic, dill, savory, thyme, chive, or basil. You can shape the butter in a roll, wrap in aluminum foil, and freeze. By freezing the butter you can cut off slices as you need them.

Bee balm can be dried and used as tea.

Herbs for teas

The controlled temperature in a drying cabinet enhances the flavor of herbs to be used in teas. Try bee balm, camomile, pennyroyal, catnip, sage, pineapple sage, hyssop, comfrey, anise, fennel, mint, and even horehound. To make tea from herbs, use 8 to 10 leaves per tea cup of boiling water and steep about 5 minutes. Experiment by blending herbs, or add citrus peel. One teaspoon of dried herb is generally equal to 1 tablespoon of the fresh herb.

Meat department

After you master the technique of curing and marinating meats, the next step is drying and smoking. It gives meat a better flavor and allows for long storage.

I hope you can rig up a little barrel smokehouse or make an old refrigerator into one. We get more pleasure out of smoking meats and have tried ham, bacon, fish, sausage, weiners, chicken, and turkey. Cure each in a brine or dry salt and then smoke according to directions.

Refrigerator smokehouse

We've converted an old refrigerator into a meat smoker. Use one that has as little plastic inside as possible. Make sure the refrigerator has shelves *(see illustration)*.

Rig up a hot plate arrangement for the bottom of the refrigerator; you'll need to cut a hole for the electric cord. You can also use a hibachi filled with charcoal. When the briquets are burning nicely, add soaked hickory chips for a dense smoke.

Cut a hole near the top of the refrigerator for a draft outlet. The top hole should have a sliding cover to adjust the draft. You'll also need a thermometer to place next to the meat.

Jerky

Everyone loves beef jerky. It is a popular treat, ideal for camping or backpacking. Jerky can be made from almost any meat, including beef, venison, or pork. If you use pork, boil the meat slices long enough to remove the red color and eliminate any chance of trichinosis developing. Generally 2 pounds of meat will yield ¾ of a pound of jerky.

Cutting with the grain, slice the meat into ⅛ to ¼ inch strips. Remove every trace of fat. Marinate 3 pounds of meat strips overnight in a solution of 1 tablespoon salt, 1 tablespoon onion powder, 1 teaspoon garlic powder, ½ teaspoon black pepper, and enough water to cover. To fully marinate, be sure to turn the slices over.

Drain the meat on paper towelling. Place on racks in the smoker or drying cabinet until quite dry. The drier it is, the longer it will keep. It is best to store jerky in the refrigerator or freezer.

You can also dry jerky in the oven. Set the oven at its lowest temperature and place the marinated strips on the rack in a single layer. Put a foil lined pan under the rack to catch any drippings. Open the oven door occasionally to cool down the oven and let some moisture escape. It will take 12 hours or more to dry the meat depending on the thickness.

Modern pemmican

Pemmican comes from an Indian word meaning "to grease." The Cree Indians of Montana and Central Canada first made pemmican. Not surprisingly, it makes a good trail food.

Pound ½ pound of jerky into a powder or grind it very fine. Add 1½

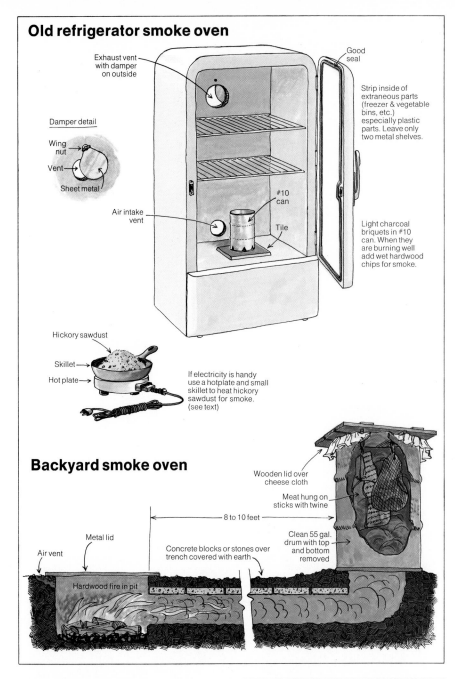

Old refrigerator smoke oven

Exhaust vent with damper on outside

Good seal

Strip inside of extraneous parts (freezer & vegetable bins, etc.) especially plastic parts. Leave only two metal shelves.

Damper detail

Wing nut

Vent

Sheet metal

Air intake vent

#10 can

Tile

Light charcoal briquets in #10 can. When they are burning well add wet hardwood chips for smoke.

Hickory sawdust

Skillet

Hot plate

If electricity is handy use a hotplate and small skillet to heat hickory sawdust for smoke. (see text)

Backyard smoke oven

Wooden lid over cheese cloth

Meat hung on sticks with twine

8 to 10 feet

Clean 55 gal. drum with top and bottom removed

Metal lid

Air vent

Concrete blocks or stones over trench covered with earth

Hardwood fire in pit

cups raisins or ground dry apricots and ¾ cup finely chopped and un-roasted nuts. Heat 2 teaspoons honey and 4 tablespoons peanut butter and blend all together. Add ¾ teaspoon cayenne powder and work it thoroughly through the pemmican. Place into little plastic bags and store in a cool, dry place.

Smoking fish

Smoking fish is a good beginner's project. There are two methods of smoking—hot smoking and cold smoking. In the hot smoking method, the fish is cooked, ready to eat, and will not keep long out of the refrigerator or freezer. In the cold smoked method, the fish, also ready to eat, dries out more and allows for much longer storage.

Hot smoking technique for fish

Clean and wash fish (any variety) thoroughly. Be sure to remove all traces of blood if you use whole fish. If you cut fillets, be sure to leave the skin on so the meat does not fall apart. Soak the fish for 30 minutes in a brine of ½ cup pickling salt to 1 quart water; drain.

Prepare a mixture of 2 pounds salt, 1 pound sugar, 1 ounce saltpeter, 1 ounce crushed black peppers, and 1 ounce crushed bay leaves. (Since the spices add flavor and do not affect the curing, you can actually spice to your heart's content.) Soak the fish in this mixture 2 to 4 hours depending on the thickness and size of the fish. After the brining, wash the fish in clear water and remove excess brine. Hang

outside in a breezy place until a thin shiny skim forms on the surface, about 3 hours.

Place the fish in a smokehouse or little smoking cabinet. Keep the fire low, smoldering for the first 8 hours. Do not let the temperature rise above 90 degrees. Now build up a dense smoke and process for 4 hours, gradually increasing the temperature to 130-150, but no higher. Cure at this temperature for 2 to 3 hours or until the fish has a glossy, brown surface.

Cool the fish for 2 to 3 hours and brush lightly with salad oil while still warm. Wrap the fish in heavy waxed paper and store in the refrigerator for immediate use or package tightly for freezing.

Cold smoking process for fish

Clean and soak the fish for 30 minutes or more in a brine of 1 cup salt to 1 gallon of water. Rinse in fresh water and drain. Thoroughly salt each fish. Pack in even layers in a box or crock, scattering more salt between the layers.

For large fish, alternate layers with ¼ inch salt. Small fish should cure for 12 hours, the larger ones for 3 days. The longer the salt brining, the longer the fish can be stored after smoking. While the fish is salted, keep in a cool place.

Remove the fish from the salt and rinse thoroughly. Scrub off all visible salt and any waste you didn't notice before. Dry the smaller fish outdoors in the shade with adequate ventilation. Place the larger fish directly into the smokehouse. Dry both until a thin skin forms on the surface (about 3 to 4 hours).

An hour or two before smoking, start a low smoldering fire. If you cure for 24 hours or more do not let the fire smoke excessively the first 12 hours. Keep the temperature at 80 degrees; never above 90 for cold smoking. Here I stress buying a thermometer, as excessive heat will destroy the flavor and quality of meat or fish.

Hang the fish or place on shelves in the smoker. After the first smoking period, build up a dense smoke and maintain until smoking is complete. Wet hickory chips create a nice, dense smoke. Keep the fire burning steadily. If the fish begins to drip fat, the temperature is too high.

Smoke fish at this low temperature for 24 hours. For a longer storage life, smoke 4 to 5 days. Store by wrapping in paper and hanging in a dry cool place. Examine for mold from time to time and remove with a clean cloth. Before using soak overnight in cold water.

Using a fruit press

The versatile fruit press makes apple cider, hard cider, vinegar, olive oil, and even cheese

Where to find it...

Because of a limitation of space and the extensive nature of wine making, we did not include it in this chapter. If you use your press for making wine, here are some excellent sources for both supplies and information:

Presque Isle Wine Making
9440 Buffalo Road
Northeast, PA 16428

Vino Corporation
Box 7498
Rochester, NY 14615

Write first and they will send you a catalog which includes the shops closest to you.

The following are some of the better books on the art of home wine making:

The Art of Making Wine — $2.50
Anderson-Hawthorne Books, Inc.
70 Fifth Avenue
New York, NY 10011

How To Make the Finest Wines at Home
Herter-Herters, Inc.
Rt. 5 — 190
Mitchell, SD 57301

Guide to Better Wine and Beer Making for Beginners
Tritton-Dover Publishing Inc.
180 Varick Street
New York, NY 10003

These books are my most useful for making cheeses:

Cheese Making at Home — $5.95
Radke-Doubleday and Company, Inc.
Garden City, NY 11530

Making Homemade Cheeses and Butter — $2.95
Hobson-Garden Way Publishers
Charlotte, VT 05445

Many mail order catalogs list their kits.

Rennet and color tablets can be ordered directly from:

Chr. Hansen's Lab., Inc.
9015 West Maple Street
Milwaukee, WI 53214

Cheese making information comes free with the rennet or coloring compound.

◊

A close up view of apple pulp in a cider press. Complete story on page 62.

Apple cider

Cider making is one of our favorite family projects. We usually have a break after the busy summer harvest, and by late September and early October, we are eager to spend a day or two making cider for winter enjoyment. On cider-making days our kitchen and yard are heavy with the aroma of the sweet crushed fruit.

Apples for cider

When you select apples for cider, the flavor of the apple is more important than the appearance. You can choose cheaper, smaller apples with blemishes. Even apples that have fallen from the tree are useable. Naturally you don't want to use apples with a lot of brown rot, but oddly shaped or uneven-sized apples are often a good bargain and do not detract from the cider's quality.

Use a variety of apples, both tart and sweet, for the best cider. We crushed Red Delicious apples and found the juice too sweet. By blending it half and half with the sharper juice from Pippin apples, we developed the correct balance. Wild apples are much too tart and must be blended with sweeter eating apples. Taste and blend until you find a suitable flavor. One bushel of apples yields approximately 2 gallons of cider.

Crushing and pressing the fruit

The easiest way to crush the fruit is to use an apple crusher. In our area you can rent them for a day or two. You can also buy crushers through mail order houses. A slower but still effective way is to run the apples through a food grinder using the coarse blade. Coarsely chop the unpeeled apples before grinding. Catch the pulp and juice run off in a glass or enamelware container. Aluminum or other unglazed containers make the apple juice bitter and turn it a dark color.

Some cider experts claim that the finest flavored cider comes from exposing the crushed pulp to the air for 24 hours prior to pressing. It does seem to have a better flavor, but we cannot find a good place to do this. There are too many ducks around our yard.

After crushing, place the pulp in a heavy jelly bag. Use a fruit press to extract the juice. Press steadily, but slowly. We burst several of my favorite jelly bags before we learned the trick of making only small turns with the press. Once you set the jelly bag of crushed fruit in the press, go on about something else, just coming back to the press occasionally to give it a turn, then leave it alone to drip

awhile. This method will give you the clearest juice. After pressing one side of the jelly bag, turn it over and press from the opposite side.

We crush inside but press the apples outside in a shady place. It is an easy matter to shake out the spent pulp right onto the compost pile, refilling the jelly bag for another pressing.

Pour the freshly pressed apple juice quickly into clean jugs or bottles and store in the refrigerator. It is ready to drink at any time.

Freshly pressed cider has a cloudy look like the product sold as natural apple juice. We like to drink it that way —it has the richest flavor. Clear apple juice however looks more beautiful and often I refrigerate the cider for several days so the sediment will settle, then rack and bottle the clear juice. Racking is a process of transferring the juice, by means of a siphon, into a new clean container, leaving the sediment at the bottom of the bottle.

When I can the cider, sometimes I let the juice clear in the refrigerator before canning. Sometimes I go ahead and can the juice and let it settle in the jars. Both methods work equally well for me and it depends largely on how much refrigerator space I have.

If you wish to keep the cider sweet for longer than a week, you need to can it, freeze it, or pasteurize it by heating to 170 degrees and holding it there for 10 minutes.

Hard cider

To make hard cider you must use the fresh unpasteurized juice. Let stand in the refrigerator a few days for the sediment to settle, then carefully pour into a crock, leaving the sediment at the bottom, or rack it. Filter the juice through several layers of cheesecloth if you want an especially clear drink. For each gallon of cider, heat ½ pound (1⅛ cups) of sugar in just enough water to dissolve the sugar. Add the sugar to the cider along with 1 package of wine or bread yeast dissolved first in a little water. Cover the crock lightly with several layers of cheesecloth, a towel, or with the lid left slightly ajar with a block of wood. Let stand at room temperature. After no more bubbling occurs, in one to two weeks, siphon the cider into sterilized wine bottles and seal with tight corks. Hard cider can be drunk in a short time and does not require long term aging.

If you bottle the cider before the fermentation has stopped, it might explode. To determine if the cider is ready for bottling, put some in a small bottle with a cork in it and place in a *(continued on page 63)*

Cider making in the Willamette Valley

Professor Willis A. Sheets of the North Willamette, Oregon, Experiment Station, tells us how to make cider with his antiquated cider mill.

"The mill was of 1872 vintage. In the early stages of its life it was used in the Missouri Ozarks. Then it was moved to Oregon via flatcar, by the New Pacific Railroad, before the turn of the century. It still operates and makes very good cider. I wouldn't say it's the most efficient machine in the world but the end product does taste very good.

"We start out with good quality fruit. I don't feel it's good to make cider out of rotten fruit or partially rotten apples. It's good to start out with a mixture of varieties which always makes a better cider than a single variety. Either Golden or Red Delicious seem to make rather poor quality cider when used by themselves. But when mixed with Jonathan, Winesap, McIntosh, or most anything, it improves considerably.

"Always wash the apples. A good way to do it is in a waterproof, metal wheelbarrow.

"The apples are put into the hopper and if they are big, they have to be squeezed through the grinder-part of the mill. This is best done with a stick and *not* with the fingers because you can come up with some skinny fingers sometimes if the apple goes through when you weren't expecting it. The fineness of the grind requires a little more manpower or horsepower, whichever you've got on the handle. It's more difficult to grind a fine grind, but by the same token you get more cider or more juice from finely ground apples.

"The slotted tub, pictured, if packed full with finely ground apples, will yield approximately 5 quarts of cider. You get only about 1 gallon of cider out of one of these tubs with coarse ground apples.

"The cider should be allowed to settle in catching basins, for awhile, before filtering. It's always a good idea to filter the cider before putting into the jug because there will be some pieces of apple skin that have fallen into the tub, and mixed into the squeezings. When allowed to set a few minutes, quite a few of these will settle out before the cider is put into the jug."

warm place. If the cork pops off, there's too much pressure and it's too early to bottle. Keep in the crock until the test cork stays in place.

Tepache Mexican pineapple cider

This slightly alcoholic drink comes from Jalisco, Mexico. Though it is called a cider, it is made with pineapple. Wash 1 large fresh pineapple and remove the leaves. Peel fruit, then cut the fruit and skin in small pieces. Using the coarse blade of the food chopper, grind the skin, fruit, and core. Place in a crock with 12 cups of water, a 2-inch piece of stick cinnamon, 10 whole cloves, and 5 whole anise seeds. Cover the crock loosely and let stand at room temperature for 48 hours.

Homemade vinegars

Vinegar takes a long time to make, but requires more patience than effort. I like to make it so I have a variety for gift giving. To make vinegar you start with freshly pressed apple juice; juice from tart apples makes the best vinegar. As when making hard cider, the juice should not be pasteurized (heated). Strain the juice through cheesecloth or filter paper and pour into a crock. Leave enough headspace for the bubbling which occurs during fermentation.

Cover with a triple layer of cheesecloth, and tie it down tightly with string. Mark the date on the side of the crock with a china marking pencil. Store in a cool dark place, such as a basement, for 4 to 6 months.

In four months, taste the vinegar to see if it is strong enough. If it is still too weak, continue to ferment and taste again in another week. Taste weekly until you like the flavor.

During fermentation a scum will form on the top. This is called the "mother." When the taste of the vinegar is right, remove the "mother" by dipping into the vinegar with a fine sieve. Strain the vinegar through cheesecloth, pour into clean bottles, and seal with bottle caps and a cap-

ping device. A bottle capper is a very inexpensive device and I find dozens of uses for it.

Save the "mother" to start another batch of vinegar. Fill a clean crock with unpasteurized apple juice, add the "mother" starter, and let it ferment. You can keep a crock of vinegar going all the time.

Do not use the homemade vinegar for canning. It is too difficult to properly determine the acid content of the vinegar in home testing methods. This is an excellent vinegar to use for salad dressing and in marinating. Or you can float home grown herbs inside of small bottles of vinegar for gifts.

Herb vinegars

Herb vinegars can be made by adding various herbs in large or small quantities, depending on your taste, to bottles of homemade vinegar. Check sprays of herbs before adding them to the vinegar, making sure there are no frayed leaves or hidden bugs, as any imperfection is magnified by the vinegar in the bottles.

Homemade fruit press and basket

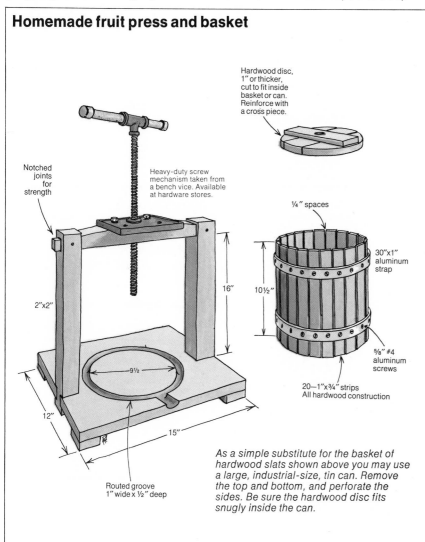

Notched joints for strength

Heavy-duty screw mechanism taken from a bench vice. Available at hardware stores.

Hardwood disc, 1" or thicker, cut to fit inside basket or can. Reinforce with a cross piece.

¼" spaces

30"x1" aluminum strap

16"

10½"

2"x2"

⅝" #4 aluminum screws

9½

12"

15"

20—1"x¾" strips
All hardwood construction

Routed groove
1" wide x ½" deep

As a simple substitute for the basket of hardwood slats shown above you may use a large, industrial-size, tin can. Remove the top and bottom, and perforate the sides. Be sure the hardwood disc fits snugly inside the can.

Small homemade fruit press

Pomace in cloth sack

For those who don't have access to the old style fruit press, there are several newer models available. From top left to right: Rival Single Action Juice-o-mat, Vita-Sphere, Acme 5001, Mehu-Maija. Bottom left to right: Miracle Pulp Ejector MJ 147, Sanyo Juicer/Blender SJ6100, Panasonic Juicer/Blender 130P.

All the models shown are electric except for the hand operated Rival Juice-o-mat and the Finnish made Mehu-Maija which extracts fruit juices by steam. The Sanyo and the Panasonic juicers double as blenders with special attachments.

The Vita-Sphere, Miracle, Sanyo and Panasonic models eject the fruit pulp into a self-contained basket, which means you can juice more fruit without having to clean the pulp out of the machine.

The electric models were tested for juicing efficiency using carrots for the test. The Acme, Miracle, Sanyo, and Panasonic all delivered approximately the same amount of juice, while the Vita-Sphere produced approximately 20 percent more juice.

Juicers courtesy Whole Earth Access Company; Mehu-Maija, Sphere Magazine.

Extracting fruit juices

Fruit	Preparing Fruit	Extracting Juice	Sugar
Apples	Wash. Use fruit juice extractor or hand press or put through food grinder, using coarsest knife.	Do not heat. Squeeze through a strong clean cloth bag; strain.	None
Apricots Nectarines Peaches	Use only firm fruit, ripe but not soft. Wash; remove any stems.	Drop fruit in boiling water, ½ to 1 inch deep; boil until soft. Put through a colander to separate skins and pits from pulp; strain.	Mix equal parts pulp, thin syrup (1 cup sugar to 4 cups water) or blend in equal part orange or grapefruit juice.
Blackberry Boysenberry Loganberry Raspberry Youngberry	Wash and crush well-ripened berries.	Heat to 175° F. Drain and squeeze through a cloth or bag; strain.	Not necessary; if desired, use 1 cup sugar to 9 cups juice.
Grapes, red	Wash; remove large stems. Fill cheese-cloth bag with quart of grapes. Immerse in gallon of rapidly boiling water for 30 seconds. Crush fruit or put through coarse food chopper.	Do not reheat. Drain and squeeze through a cloth or bag; strain.	None
Grapes, purple	Wash; remove large stems; crush fruit or put through coarse food chopper. Avoid crushing seeds.	Heat to 160° F. Drain and squeeze through a cloth or bag; strain.	None
Grapes, white	Wash; remove large stems; crush fruit or put through coarse food chopper. Avoid crushing seeds.	Do not heat. Drain and squeeze through a cloth or bag; strain.	None
Strawberries	Wash, hull and crush.	Heat to 175° F. Drain and squeeze through a cloth or bag; strain.	I cup sugar to 3 cups juice. If blended with other berry juice, 1 cup sugar, 9 of juice.
Cherries, (sweet or sour)	Wash, stem, pit and crush or put through food chopper.	Heat to 160° F. Drain and squeeze through a cloth or bag; strain.	Not necessary; if desired, 1 cup sugar to 9 cups juice.
Cherries, white	Wash, stem, pit, and crush or put through food chopper.	Do not heat. Drain and squeeze through a cloth or bag; strain.	Not necessary; if desired, 1 cup sugar to 9 cups juice.
Oranges Lemons Grapefruit	Navel oranges are not recommended for canning juice; if used, cut out navel end before reaming.	Do not heat. Use any type reamer except press type; avoid pressing oil or juice from peel; do not remove pulp.	None
Plums	Use firm, rich-flavored, well-colored plums. Wash, crush, and add 1 quart water to each 2 pounds of plums.	Heat at about 180° F. until soft. Drain and squeeze through a cloth or bag; strain.	Add sugar to taste—about 1 cup sugar to 4 cups of juice.
Rhubarb	Wash stalks; cut into 4-inch lengths. Add 2 quarts water for each 10 pounds rhubarb.	Heat until water begins to boil. Drain and squeeze through a cloth or bag; strain.	Add 1 cup sugar to 2 quarts (8 cups) juice.
Tomatoes	Use well-ripened tomatoes deep in color.	Put through a fine colander; add salt to taste.	None

Try using tarragon sprays, garlic, dill, rosemary, basil, orange-mint, burnet, or any other favorite herb. A long spray that goes from the top to the bottom of the bottle makes an attractive sight. Let the vinegar stand for 5 to 6 weeks, long enough for the herb to flavor the vinegar completely.

Save old salad dressing bottles or similar fancy bottles for the vinegars you want to give as gifts; old cruets can be used for an elegant touch.

You can experiment flavoring vinegar with herb seeds, such as dill or anise, but crush the seeds first. Warm the vinegar before pouring over the seeds to extract the most flavor.

Some people suggest that homemade vinegars are not pale enough in color to see the herbs floating inside. If your homemade vinegars are dark in color you can solve this problem by using half homemade vinegar and half white distilled vinegar.

Canned fruit juices

If you are going to can or bottle fruit juices you don't have to add sugar to the juice, the juice can be sweetened to taste just before use. By leaving out the sugar in canned juices you have an added bonus, in that the unsweetened juice can be made into jelly at a later date.

Storing the juice in jars and bottles allows any remaining sediment to settle. If you make jelly with this juice you get an extra clear and brilliant product, especially if you are careful not to disturb any of the remaining sediment. No matter how well you try to filter the juice at first, it seems that there is always a little sediment remaining. By canning the juice and allowing the remaining sediment to settle, you can get the clearest possible juice.

Clear juice using paper tissues

Place ten sheets of white, unscented paper tissues (the kind that *will* disintegrate when wet) in a saucepan. Add two quarts hot water and stir with a spoon to break up the paper tissues. Turn the whole mass into a big strainer and shake out the excess water, but do not squeeze.

Put the tissue mass into the saucepan again, and add 8 cups crushed berries. Bring to a boil, stirring constantly. Cook just until the fruit is tender.

Place the fruit and paper tissue mixture in a jelly bag. When cool enough to handle, squeeze out the juice by force until the remaining pulp is quite

dry. Note that this is contrary to the instructions I gave you before which said *not* to squeeze the jelly bag. If you squeeze the jelly bag using the normal method of extracting juices, you get a mucky liquid; with the paper tissue method it will result in a perfectly clear liquid, even if you squeeze the bag with considerable pressure.

Back to the berries; you ought to have about six cups of berry juice. The juice should be heated to the scalding point now, and put into bottles and sealed. Process the bottles in a simmering water-bath for ten minutes (see page 26). The juice may be used as a drink, or to make jelly or syrup later. The paper tissue method makes clear, bright juices.

Most of the paper tissues on the market today advertise 'wet strength' and other indications of how well they hold together, no matter how waterlogged they get. Shop around until you find the soggiest brand, with no perfume added, which spoils the aroma of the fresh fruit.

When I am in a hurry I use the fastest method, straining the juice through a filter paper or a bag, squeezing when necessary to hurry the process. For the juices and jellies I plan to enter in the Fair, however, I always use the paper tissue method. For home use, it really isn't necessary to have absolutely clear juices and jellies.

Store homemade juices in a cool, dry place to preserve the fresh flavor, color and vitamin content. Properly prepared juices will *not spoil,* even when stored in a warm place, but they will lose some flavor, color and vitamins if they are stored at temperatures over 70°.

Spiced blackberry juice

Mash and strain unheated, ripe blackberries through a food mill. To each quart of juice you get, add two cups sugar. Make a little spice bag of cheesecloth and fill with 4½ teaspoons nutmeg, 1 tablespoon whole cinnamon pieces, 1 tablespoon whole cloves and a piece of mace.

Simmer juice and spice bag over low heat for 20 minutes. Remove spice and stir in 2 tablespoons vanilla. Pour into hot sterilized jars, seal, and process in simmering water bath for 10 minutes. (See page 26)

Cranberry juice

Boil 4 cups cranberries in 4 cups water for 15 minutes. Place berries in jelly bag and let drip slowly, without squeezing the bag. Take the pulp from the bag, after you have gotten as

much juice as possible from it, and put in a kettle, add 1½ cups water and boil for two minutes. Place pulp back in the jelly bag to extract the remaining juice.

Mix the two batches of juice together, for every two cups cranberry juice, add ½ cup sugar. Bring to a boil and pour into sterilized jars, seal and process 10 minutes in a simmering water bath. (See page 26)

The fastest method for fruit juices

Use this method for berries or grapes. Sterilize quart jars and lids. Pour one cup of fruit, and ½ cup sugar into the jar and fill to the brim with boiling water and seal.

You end up with spent fruit in the bottom of the jar, but by steeping the fruit in the water with the sugar, right in the jar, an excellent juice is produced. I do several dozen quart jars of grape juice this way each year.

Pour very carefully for the clearest juice. When you come to the fruit in the bottom of the jar you can put it into a collander or a little strainer and press it to use for a purée. This leftover fruit can also be mixed with gelatin desserts, or save up several days' worth and use as a base for sherbet.

Blending juices

Sometimes blending homemade juices makes a better product. Apricot or peach juice mixed with orange or grapefruit is delicious. The citrus juice balances out the extra sweetness of the apricot or peach juice.

Add carbonated water or ginger ale to homemade juices for delicious punches. Try different blends of mixed fruit juices and make note of your favorite blends. In the future you can mix the fruit that made the best blend together before you extract the juice. If the different types of fruit are pressed together, their flavors blend better during storage.

Tomato juice cocktail

To each quart of freshly extracted tomato juice add two teaspoons salt, ½ teaspoon grated onion, 1 teaspoon grated celery, ½ teaspoon prepared horseradish, 1½ teaspoons lemon juice, and ¼ teaspoon Worcestershire sauce. A really delicious tomato juice blend. Can be used straight or for mixed drinks.

Alternate tomato juice blends are as follows: Four parts tomato juice to one part sauerkraut juice, or try 8 parts tomato juice to one part celery juice. Try four parts tomato juice, 1 part celery juice to 1 part carrot juice.

You can add small amounts of onion juice to any of these blends for yet another variation. Be sure to label each of the recipes right on the jars so you can decide which are your favorites.

Making cheese

Unless one has an inexpensive source of milk from a cow, I have always felt that cheesemaking was not necessarily a money saving project. It is very satisfying to make however, and of course, homemade cheese has that special flavor because you made it yourself.

You can make many different kinds of cheese and the processes are basically the same—the watery part of the milk, the whey, separates from the firmer part, the curd, by the action of rennet, or heat ,or both. Rennet is a substance that speeds curdling and prevents the formed curd from breaking up easily. After the whey is drained from the curd, the curd is made into cheese. There are exceptions to this, such as ricotta which is made from the whey.

Most cheese is made from cow's milk, but goat's milk can be used as well. Cheese can be made from skimmed milk, whole milk, or a combination of both. Many cheesemakers feel that the milk causes as many variables in the flavor of cheese as grapes do in wine making. You can get a difference in flavor just from what the cow has eaten. One gallon of milk will yield about ¾ pound of cheese.

Equipment

The equipment for making cheese is surprisingly simple; you may have most of it at home. You will need several yards of cheesecloth, cheese rennet tablets (available in drug stores), a dairy thermometer, and a double boiler arrangement made from one big kettle that fits inside a larger kettle. Do not use galvanized metal or aluminum containers to hold the milk.

A stainless steel container is best, but you can use any acid-resistant enamelware or a heavily-tinned container.

For a cheese mold you will need a #10 can or a smooth-sided, 3 pound coffee can. Don't use a can that has little rings or ridges on the sides. Remove the top and bottom of the can to form a hollow cylinder. Using a jig saw, cut a 1-inch thick piece of wood into a circle that will just fit loosely inside the can. This is called the follower.

Warming and curdling the milk

For my double boiler I use two canning kettles; one is large and the other is enormous. I put a rack on the bottom of the enormous one, fill it one-third full of water, and put the large canning kettle inside on the rack.

Pour 4 gallons of milk into the inner kettle and fasten the dairy thermometer on the inside of the kettle. Heat over hot water until the milk reaches 90 degrees. Turn off the heat. Add 2 cups buttermilk to the milk, stir well, and let stand for 2 hours. Turn on heat to medium high, and stirring occasionally, heat milk until it reaches 88 to 90 degrees. Turn off heat and leave milk at that temperature.

Now dissolve ½ of one of the cheese rennet tablets in a little cold water and add the mixture to the milk. Stir well for 30 seconds, then let the milk rest without stirring or shaking for 45 minutes. The temperature should remain at 88 to 90 degrees during this time.

Cutting the curd

After 45 minutes, use a long bladed knife to cut down through the cheese. Cut parallel lines 1-inch apart in both horizontal and perpendicular directions. Then hold the knife at an angle and cut into the cheese diagonally, making the long skinny columns into 1 inch cubes.

Let the cut curd stand for 10 minutes. Turn the heat on and let it steadily rise to 104 degrees, occasionally stirring very gently. On my electric range, a setting of medium will reach 104 degrees in about an hour. Turn the heat off and maintain a temperature of 104 degrees for 1 hour, stirring occasionally. While the mixture sits, the cubes will solidify. You can notice the greenish colored whey as the cubes separate.

At the end of the hour, remove the whey with a spoon or dipper and save

Cutting the curd

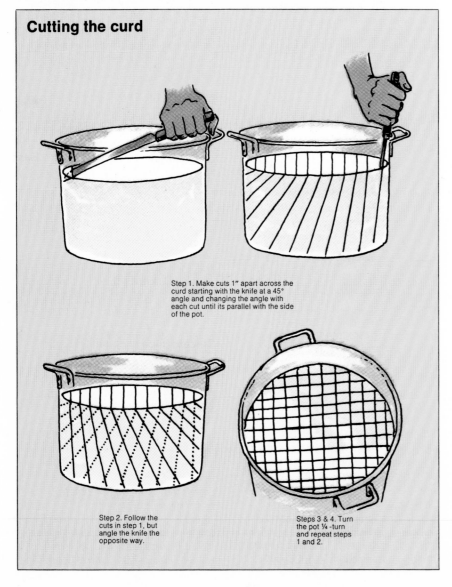

Step 1. Make cuts 1″ apart across the curd starting with the knife at a 45° angle and changing the angle with each cut until its parallel with the side of the pot.

Step 2. Follow the cuts in step 1, but angle the knife the opposite way.

Steps 3 & 4. Turn the pot ¼ -turn and repeat steps 1 and 2.

to make ricotta cheese (recipe follows). After the whey is removed, salt the cubes with 4 tablespoons salt and stir well.

Pressing the cheese

Line the hollow coffee can with a double thickness of cheesecloth. I hold the cheesecloth in place with 4 clothes pins, one on each quarter of the can. Pack the cheese down into the coffee can and fold the top edges of the cheesecloth over the top. Trim cheesecloth if it is too bulky. Fit the wooden disk (the follower) down inside of the can on top of the cheese and place the whole thing on the floor of the fruit press.

Fit the pusher part of the press down on top of the follower. Slowly press the cheese, gradually forcing out more and more of the whey. I leave it and come back at intervals, turning the press a little bit tighter each time. If you press too quickly, the cheese becomes lopsided, and you may need to repack it.

After 45 minutes of pressing, remove the can from the press. Make sure the cheesecloth is smooth. Turn the can upside down, replace the follower on top, and return to the press so the second side gets an equal pressing. Leave it in the press overnight. If you do not have a press, you can use 3 to 4 bricks on top of the follower. You have to make sure the bricks are always level.

Drying and aging the cheese

In the morning, remove the cheese from the can. Rewrap if the cheesecloth is wrinkled. Place the cheese on a board or other flat surface and let it stand in a well ventilated spot to dry. Turn the cheese several times daily so it will dry on both sides.

The cheese should dry in about four days. Leave the cheesecloth covering on it, then dip it very carefully in melted paraffin, turning to cover all sides. Let cheese stand on waxed paper until paraffin is dry and solid. If you're short on paraffin, use surplus candles. You might cut the cheese into pieces before paraffining and age each piece separately.

Store the paraffin coated cheese at 50 degrees. I write the date on the cheese with a marking pen so that I know the age of the cheese. In a month, test one piece of cheese to see if it is sharp enough. This cheese is like a semi-hard, mild, white Cheddar.

Although cheese can be made in a variety of improvised presses (see text), here a special cheese press is used. Finished cheeses are wrapped in cheesecloth, paraffined, and stored at 50 degrees to improve flavor and texture.

The longer you let it age, the sharper the flavor becomes.

I realize that this seems like a rather big undertaking, but this is a fairly simple recipe and a good one to learn the basic techniques.

Ricotta from the leftover whey

Add 1 quart fresh whole milk to the whey leftover from 10 quarts of milk. Stirring, heat over medium heat to 200 degrees. When the curd begins to rise and form on the top, quickly stir in ½ cup vinegar. Continue stirring and as the curd reforms, use a small strainer and skim off the ricotta. Salt to taste and drain for a few hours in a cloth bag or strainer. I use ricotta in lasagna or on pizza combined with other cheeses.

Grinding Grains

A satisfying way to get the most flavor and nutrition from a variety of whole grains

A special grain grinding attachment works well for grinding small amounts of flour. Many different grain mills are now available for home use.

When properly stored, *whole* grains keep a very long time. After the grain is ground it begins to lose its flavor in about a months time. If you grind the grain yourself, as you need it, you can be certain of the freshest flavor.

Grinding your own grains has become increasingly popular with the availability of home grain mills. Storing whole grain at home, and grinding it just prior to use not only insures the freshest flavor, it is also the best way to use all the nutrients.

You can buy any number of grains (if you don't raise them yourself), such as wheat, rye, corn, and oats. Beside the sources listed below, bulk grains are available from health food stores, feed stores, or grain mill stores.

Cleaning the grain

In most cases it is necessary to clean the grain, especially if you raise it yourself. The grain still contains chaff and weed seeds and needs to be winnowed. The easiest way to do this is to drop the grain from a height from one container to another. Set up an electric fan to create a breeze around the falling material so the heavy grains will fall straight into the second container while the lighter chaff and other seeds will blow away. Then pick over the grain to be sure all the extraneous material has been eliminated.

Storage of wheat and other grains

Store the cleaned grain in a new metal or plastic garbage can. Be careful with the latter, since some plastics have a strong odor which might be absorbed by the grains. Store the container in a cool dry place. If the grain is completely dry no insects can reproduce in it. Keep away from any odorous products such as kerosene, gasoline, or even onions. Any container used to store grain should have a tight fitting lid.

If you store grains for more than a year, check them several times and change containers. This aerates the grain as you pour it from one container to the other. Try to use up all the grain before the new crop comes in.

Grinding grains

Grain can be ground fine for cereals, very fine for flour for bread making, and extra coarse for pilaf and cracked wheat. You can grind grain in an electric grain mill, a coffee mill (slow, but sure), or a hand mill; quite popular now and widely available.

Always store any ground grain in the refrigerator or freezer if you are not going to use it right away. The ground grain contains the germ of the grain as well as other parts of the kernel. The germ has a high fat content, and after a few days, without the additives used in commercial flours for longer storage, the taste becomes flat. If the temperature becomes too warm, the ground grain will actually turn rancid. The easiest way to use the grain is to grind it as you need it.

Buying wheat

There are many varieties of wheat but generally they fall into two categories—hard and soft wheat. Only hard wheat contains enough gluten for bread making. Soft wheat can be used for cakes, pilaf, and sprouting (see page 75).

I accidentally bought soft wheat one time for making bread. When the first loaf of bread didn't rise, I purchased pure gluten flour from a health food store to add to the soft wheat flour. One tablespoon of gluten flour mixed with each cup of soft wheat flour makes an acceptable bread. Try this solution if the only wheat available in your area is the soft variety.

Mariel's whole wheat bread

My secret for moist and tender whole wheat bread is to soak the freshly ground flour overnight. This softens the bran, which is the water repellant part of the whole grain. The liquid called for in the bread recipe can be either potato water, vegetable cooking water, milk, or water. Milk gives the finished loaf a softer texture and water gives a crunchier texture.

To make three 2-pound loaves, mix 12 cups freshly ground whole wheat flour, ½ cup honey, ⅓ cup salad oil, 2 tablespoons salt, and 5½ cups hot potato or vegetable water, or milk. Let stand overnight in a covered bowl.

In the morning sprinkle 2 packages of active dry yeast in ¼ cup warm water and let stand until dissolved. Add yeast to dough mixture, and work it in thoroughly by hand. Let the dough rest for 10 minutes, and then knead thoroughly for 10 minutes or until dough is smooth and springy. If the dough sticks badly, add a tiny bit of white flour or grease to your hands. The less flour you work in, the lighter the bread.

Mariel's whole wheat bread (for recipe see page 69), made even more delicious using freshly ground grain. Recipe makes three loaves, one to eat right away, two to freeze.

Place the dough in a large greased bowl, turning to grease all sides. Let rise in a warm place until doubled in bulk, about 1 hour. Punch down and let rest a few minutes while you grease 3 bread pans. Use shortening, not oil for greasing the pans.

Divide the dough evenly into 3 parts, shape into loaves, and place in bread pans. Lightly grease the tops and let rise in a warm place until *nearly* doubled, about 30 minutes.

Place the bread pans in a cold oven and turn to 325 degrees. The bread should be done in about an hour. Tap the sides of one of the pans. The bread should have a hollow sound when done.

For a brown, crispy crust, turn the hot bread out of the pans and rest directly on the oven rack. Turn off the oven and let the bread sit in the cooling oven a few minutes. Check to prevent burning.

Bulghour

You can make your own bulghour at home, sometimes called cracked wheat bulgur when sold commercially. It has a nutty flavor and chewy texture, and is a favorite in Middle Eastern cooking.

Cover whole wheat berries (the name for the whole grain) with water and let stand overnight. Place in a pot, cover, and simmer until the kernels are tender and swollen to at least twice their original size, about 45 minutes. If you do not soak the grain overnight, it takes 3 hours to cook. Drain any liquid remaining in the pan and spread the wheat in single layers on cooky sheets. Place in a 200

degree oven until very dry. This takes several hours.

Any grain must be absolutely dry when grinding. Grind the cooked and dried grain in a mill. For pilaf it should be coarse and for cereal a bit finer.

You can steam bulghour and use it as a substitute for rice or potatoes or make it into poultry dressing. Try it as a meat extender or as a filler with ground lamb and ground beef in stuffed peppers.

Pilaf

Melt 4 tablespoons butter or margarine in a heavy pan. Break up and add ½ cup vermicelli and brown slightly. Add ½ minced onion, and stirring, brown lightly. Add 1 cup medium fine bulghour (cracked toasted wheat), and sauté for several minutes. Pour in 2 cups boiling beef or chicken stock or 2 bouillon cubes dissolved in 2 cups hot water. Season to taste with salt and pepper. Cover and simmer over low heat for 20 minutes.

When the water is absorbed, remove from heat and gently stir with a fork to fluff the mixture. Cover again and bake in a 375 degree oven for 15 minutes to dry slightly. You can leave the pilaf for a longer time by lowering the oven to 200 degrees.

Home made hot cereals

Now that we have learned to toast and grind our own grains, we enjoy quite a variety of homemade cereals; they're nutritious, economical, and a good way to start the day.

I cook the cereal in a double boiler, which prevents sticking, starting it the night before we are going to have it. I put the grain in the top of the double boiler, add the right amount of water for the grain I am using, add a little salt, and bring to a boil. After it has been brought to boil, I turn off the stove and let the cereal soak overnight. This advance preparation shortens the cooking time considerably in the morning. Serve with honey or brown sugar.

Homemade hot cereal mix

Mix 1 pound steel cut oats (not the instant type), 1 pound soy grits, 1 pound rye grits, and 1 pound bulghour (cracked toasted wheat). Cover tightly and store in a cool place.

To use, boil in water. Use 3 parts water to 1 part cereal. Salt to taste. Cook for 20 to 30 minutes. Use a double boiler to prevent sticking.

Cream of wheat, rice, or rye

Place whole wheat berries, rice, or rye-grain in an *ungreased* deep frying pan. Heat over medium heat, shaking the pan to prevent scorching. Heat the grain long enough to toast—you'll know the smell when it is toasted. Grind in a grain mill making it the degree of fineness you prefer. Prepare as you would hot cereal.

Cracked wheat cereal

Cook 1 cup cracked wheat in 4 cups water and 1 teaspoon salt for 30 minutes at night. Cover and let stand overnight. Cook for 30 minutes the next morning and serve.

Whole wheat cereal

Mix 1 cup whole wheat berries with 2 cups water and 1 teaspoon salt in a deep well cooker or a crock pot. Cook overnight or for 12 hours on a low heat.

Cream of brown rice cereal

Wash and drain 2 cups brown rice in cold water. Cook in a dry skillet, shaking steadily, until the rice is *completely* dry (about 5 minutes). Grind into powder in a grain mill. Cook in 1 cup water to each 3 tablespoons ground cereal. Add a dash of salt.

Corn meal mush

Use freshly ground cornmeal for this. Grind dry corn in a grain mill. Mix 2 cups cornmeal in 7 cups cold water in a heavy saucepan. Add 1 teaspoon salt. Bring to a boil, and stirring, cook until thick. Steam it, covered, over boiling water for 15 minutes or more. Stir frequently. Eat some of the mush for breakfast and pour the rest, while still hot, into a small greased bread pan. Let it cool and then refrigerate until very cold. Slice it thin and fry the slices in butter on both sides. Serve with some of your homemade fruit syrups.

Homemade hominy

There are other interesting uses for grains. This year we grew hominy corn for the first time and made our own hominy. If you like hominy you might enjoy making your own.

Lye hominy

Place 2 quarts shelled dry white or yellow field corn or hominy corn in an *enameled* or *stainless steel* pan. Add 8 quarts water and 2 ounces of lye. Remember to be extra careful with lye, and do not use an aluminum pan. Boil the corn gently for 30 minutes or until the hulls loosen, and then cool for 20 minutes.

Carefully rinse off the lye, changing the water several times. Remove the dark tips from the kernels with your fingers.

Cover the hominy with water and boil for 5 minutes. Change the water and boil again. Repeat four more times and then cook the kernels until they are soft, about 45 minutes.

You can freeze the hominy or can it according to the directions of your steam pressure canner. If you can the hominy, cook it for 30 minutes first rather than 45. It will finish cooking during the processing time.

Lime hominy

Look for the powdered lime for this process in a hardware store. Dissolve 4 heaping tablespoons powdered lime in 4 quarts water in an enameled or stainless steel pan. Add 2 quarts of dry field corn. Stir well and cook over a low heat until the hulls loosen from the kernels. Remove from heat, drain, and wash the hominy in several changes of water until all the lime is removed and the water runs clear. This will keep for two weeks in the refrigerator. For longer storage, can or freeze.

Baked hominy

Beat ½ cup milk with 1 tablespoon melted butter and 1 egg. Combine with 1 cup cooked, drained hominy. Add ½ teaspoon salt and a pinch of pepper. Pour into a buttered baking dish and bake in a 350 degree oven until firm and brown. Serve in place of potatoes.

Baked hominy grits and cheese

Drain and dry the hominy, if you want, in the sun or in a dehydrator. To make hominy grits, grind the well dried hominy in a grain mill.

Sauté 1 small chopped onion in 2 tablespoons butter until clear. In a heavy saucepan, boil 2 cups water. Slowly add a little salt and ½ cup hominy grits. Reduce the heat and cook for 3 minutes or until mixture is thick. Remove from heat and add the sautéed onion, ½ teaspoon Tabasco sauce, a dash of pepper, and ¾ pound grated Cheddar cheese. Fold in 2 stiffly beaten egg whites, then turn mixture into a lightly greased casserole. Sprinkle with another ¼ pound of grated Cheddar cheese. Bake in 400 degree oven for 30 minutes. Serves 6.

Masa for tortillas

After you make hominy, you can turn it into *masa,* a moist dough used to make Mexican tortillas. Drain cooked hominy and run it through the food grinder three times using the fine blade. (Remember not to use a grain mill for this.) If the ground hominy seems dry, add a little water. The dough should hold together well.

Break off pieces of dough and roll into balls the size of a large walnut. Form tortillas with a tortilla press or place dough between two pieces of waxed paper and roll out with a rolling pin. Bake on an ungreased griddle or in a heavy frying pan over medium-high heat until dry and flecked with brown. Serve while still warm or use to make enchiladas or tacos.

Foods, wild and tame

Recipes to tame *wild* foods, and to discover some of the more interesting tame ones, plus the "how to" on making soap.

◁

A number of plants, seeds, and flowers, not usually thought of as edible, can be made into delicious and healthful products.

Left, top and bottom:
Rose hips form on wild and cultivated varieties of rose plants, if the flowers are left to mature. Can be made into a syrup, rich in vitamin C. (See page 73)

Top right:
Wild berries and their tame cousins are a special summer treat, eaten fresh or preserved in jams or jellies.

Bottom right:
Squash blossoms can be stuffed with meat or cheese, or fried in a tempura-like batter.

Out beyond the garage, in a nearby swamp, or on a wooded trail lies a whole world of unusual foods. Whether you find a liking for pigweed, sweet grass, day lily, or paw paw (which some claim tastes like bananas and peaches), the search for wild foods can be fun and rewarding.

At one time, the search for wild edible plants was a trial and error procedure with the possibility that an error could cost the experimenter his life.

Considering that the days have passed when such information was handed down from generation to generation, the best way to utilize wild plants and herbs today is to buy the best book available on the subject. The most useful books on the subject are ones which contain plenty of identifying photographs or illustrations. I have found Adrienne Crowhurst's *The Weed Cookbook* particularly helpful, with over two-hundred color pages of edible and inedible wild plants.

Carry the identification book whenever you go on an excursion into the wilds and use the key to identify unfamiliar plants. *Above all* use caution and be absolutely certain that *all* parts of the plant in question are edible.

Wild berries

Wild berries abound in many areas and are free for the picking. In some places the berries have escaped from tame plantings and cover acres of land. Wild blackberries are especially thorny, so wear a long sleeve shirt and gloves. The berries are usually smaller than the tame varieties, and take longer to pick.

At the risk of sounding sentimental, all the extra time and effort becomes worthwhile when on a cold day, in the dead of winter, you open a jar of wild blackberry jam and the memories of that summer afternoon spent in the berry patch by the creek all come back to you; some claim it even makes the end product taste that much better.

If wild berries are found growing next to a public road, be sure and wash them thoroughly when you get home. In many places the state road service sprays the areas next to the road with a weed killer, and it is possible that the berries have been sprayed as well.

Vitamin C rose hip syrup for children

The English make their own vitamin C syrup and give their children 2 teaspoons daily throughout the winter to guard against colds. If you allow your rose bushes to form seed pods (hips)

here's a good way to put them to use.

Mince coarsely 3 pounds of rose hips and boil in 11¼ cups water in a saucepan. Remove and let steep for 15 minutes. Pour into a jelly bag and let drip until thoroughly drained. Put the pulp from the bag into a pan, add 5 cups boiling water, and set aside for 15 minutes. Drain the juice off from this mixture, combine with the juice from the jelly bag, and boil down to about half the original measure (about 6 cups). Add 3 cups sugar, boil for 5 minutes, bottle, and cap.

Capers

Capers are called for in many recipes and add a zing to everything from veal to tartar sauce. You can make homemade imitation capers using the buds from the common nasturtium plant. The buds should be in the green stage, just before they start to swell and develop the flowers.

Gather the buds fresh and cover with a brine of 1 cup salt to 2 quarts water. Cover with a weight (such as a plate) so that all the buds are immersed in the brine and cure for 24 hours. Remove and soak in cold water for an hour. Drain and pack the buds into small, hot sterilized jars. Pour boiling vinegar over the buds and seal. Process in a hot-water-bath for 10 minutes. These imitation capers should be aged for six weeks to develop the characteristic caper flavor.

Pine nuts

Harvesting pine nuts is an exciting autumn outing. The pine nuts you see sold commercially are most often from the Piñon pine. Piñon pines are found primarily in the western states. Other pine trees with edible nuts, but with a wider adaptation are the Stone, Coulter, Korean, Torrey, Swiss, and Sugar pines. The pine nuts usually ripen in August and September and fall a month or two later. They are ready to harvest as soon as the kernels loosen and fall.

Wild animals enjoy them also, so you should shake the trees and harvest the nuts before someone or something else beats you to them.

The Indians put the green pine cones onto firepits and roasted them until the nuts fell out. You could try this somewhat tricky method, but generally people just shake the trees with poles, letting the nuts fall onto ground covers spread underneath the tree.

Most people hunt for pine nuts in Forest Service or Bureau of Land Management land. There may be a local permit required, so inquire first. Pine nuts are delicious raw or toasted.

For the birds

Make homemade feeding cakes for birds by melting 1½ cups suet. Mix well with ¼ cup sugar, ½ cup peanut butter, ½ cup flour, ½ cup cornmeal, ½ cup oatmeal, and enough bird seed mixture to hold it all together. Mold in a pan or a flower pot. When hard take out of container and hang out for winter birds to enjoy.

Scented geraniums used for baking

Place several lovely scented geranium leaves across the bottom of a well greased cake pan. Pour in the cake batter carefully so you won't disturb the leaves. Invert the cake after cooling and sprinkle the bottom of the cake with sifted powdered sugar. Carefully remove the leaves, leaving their outline in the sugar. The scent will be noticeable in the cake and the outline of the leaves makes an interesting decoration. Rose geranium leaves are commonly used; other aromatic leaves such as lemon verbena or mint work well, but leave a less noticeable outline.

Acorn bread

Make acorn flour by boiling whole acorns for at least 2 hours. Change the water each time it turns light brown in color. Boiling will remove the bitterness from the acorns. After boiling, during which the acorns turn dark brown, roast them in the oven at 350 degrees for 1 hour.

To make the flour, grind in a mill and dry again in the oven for 30 minutes. Re-grind for a very fine flour.

    2 packages active dry yeast
    ⅓ cup lukewarm water
    2 cups warm water
    ⅓ cup honey
    2 teaspoons salt
    2 tablespoons salad oil
    4⅔ cups acorn flour

1. Dissolve the dry yeast in lukewarm water.

2. When dissolved, add 2 cups warm water, honey, salt, oil, and acorn flour. Mix. Cover the bowl and let rise for 2 hours in a warm place.

3. Knead for 10 minutes.

4. Shape into 2 small loaves and place in small greased bread pans. Let rise again for another 2 hours.

5. Bake for 30 minutes in a 375 degree oven. Remove from the oven and brush with a little melted butter. Acorn meal has no gluten which accounts for the long rising period and the extra amount of yeast.

For variety use 2 or 3 cups acorn flour and the rest wheat, or white flour. The acorns have a pleasant, nutty flavor. They're delicious boiled and then roasted. You can easily remove the shells by making slits with a sharp knife and then peel.

Parched corn

Regular corn kernels can be dried, removed from the cobs, and toasted in a light coat of oil, but field corn makes big lovely parched corns, more like the popular commercial brands. Toast field corn kernels in a heavy pan with a little oil. Stir or shake continuously. The kernels are done when they turn a lovely golden brown. Salt to taste.

Indian corn pone

    1 cup bright red, blue, or black
      cornmeal
    ½ teaspoon salt
    1 teaspoon baking powder
    2 tablespoons salad oil
    ½ cup milk

1. Mix cornmeal, salt, baking powder, oil, and milk.

2. Drop the batter from a tablespoon into a large, heavy greased skillet. Shape into little cakes or pones.

3. Brown well on both sides and serve hot with butter.

Blue cornbread

Crusty, blue cornbread is typical of Navaho cooking.

    2 cups blue cornmeal
    1 cup all-purpose white flour
    1 teaspoon soda
    1 teaspoon salt
    2 eggs, beaten
    2 cups buttermilk
    2 tablespoons sugar
    2 tablespoons melted butter

1. Mix the blue cornmeal, flour, soda, and salt together.

2. In another bowl mix the beaten eggs, buttermilk, and sugar.

3. Mix both mixtures together lightly and then add the melted butter.

4. Pour into a greased 9-inch square pan and bake in a 425 degree oven for 20-25 minutes or until well browned and crusty.

Fried squash blossoms

Pick the squash blossoms just before they open completely. Dip in a light batter made from ⅓ cup milk, 1 teaspoon flour, ¼ teaspoon salt, and a dash or two of pepper. Fry in hot oil until a light golden brown. Drain on brown paper and serve immediately. This makes enough batter to coat approximately one dozen squash blossoms.

Wild plants and seeds

If you watch carefully on your hikes and outings, and take an identification book along, it won't take long before you have mastered many new plants. The following list contains a few of the more easily identifiable and widespread wild plants.

Mustard seeds are easily recognized by their odor and looks. They grow abundantly in fields and alongside the roadways and have brilliant yellow flowers. The flowers are four petaled and the plants have little seed pods containing the mustard seeds. You can grind these and add vinegar and water to make table mustard. The young early spring mustard greens are good as a first harvest green vegetable.

The weed *Queen Anne's Lace* can be used for the seeds which will add a carroty flavor to stew.

In addition to the wild seeds I gather each year, I let some of my tame varieties go to seed so I have some for culinary use. Particular favorites are dill, cumin, and coriander. Don't forget to let one celery plant go to seed. One plant provides enough celery seed to use in pickling recipes later in the year.

The small new leaves of wild chicory make a nice cooked vegetable and can be added raw to salad. The roots are sometimes roasted and then ground and used as a coffee substitute or additive.

Dandelion shoots are good in early spring, while the boiled roots will keep for later use. The greens are very good.

Wild Jerusalem artichokes can be sliced and eaten raw or steamed, peeled, and served as you would potatoes.

During early spring and late fall wild water cress and winter cress are excellent as salad greens or cooked. By mid-summer they are too bitter and strong for most tastes.

The weed Curled Dock is one of the earliest spring wild vegetables. The stems can be peeled and added to salad. Dock is sometimes mistaken for wild rhubarb. The leaves of the dock can be safely eaten, while the leaves of the common rhubarb cannot.

Cattail stalks have a delicious heart near the center of the stalks close to the plant.

During the time you are learning which plants are safe for you to eat, emphasize to your children not to ever eat wild things without your permission. There are many houseplants, garden plants, and bulbs, which are highly toxic, particularly to children. Now is a good time to teach them caution.

After you learn to identify several wild vegetables, try this method for cooking the greens. Pick only the tender young greens; the older greens are often bitter and must be cooked and drained several times. Rinse several times, lifting the greens out of the water, instead of draining, so the dirt is left on the bottom of the rinsing pan.

Cook in a very small amount of water or steam to retain all the vitamins. As with all greens, the cooking reduces size, so start with a healthy amount.

Some people enjoy the flavor of wild greens cooked with bacon and bacon grease. Add sautéed bacon bits and the grease in small amounts to lightly cooked greens.

Become a kitchen farmer

"If you plant them over-night, by morning they grow right up to the sky." Bean seller to Jack.

You can have a tiny farm in your kitchen. It's products require little space and grow independent of the outside weather. The produce can be harvested daily and its servings cost less than one cent each. Your kitchen crop is rich in vitamins and delicious raw or cooked. If you sprout beans and other seeds indoors you can become a productive "kitchen farmer."

Sprouts are inexpensive and easy to grow. They are as nutritious as meat and as rich in vitamin C as fresh fruit. The vitamin content of the seed is increased with sprouting; vitamin C can increase 500 percent and B_2 1300 percent. Folic acid, niacin, riboflavin, and pyridox also increase dramatically. Vitamins A, E, and K go up in varying amounts. In simple terms fats and starches are converted into vitamins, simple sugars, and proteins as they absorb air and water. This vitamin multiplication is so impressive, it is a wonder more people do not take advantage of the process.

Seeds are divided into two basic parts—the embryo and the endosperm. The embryo is a miniature replica of a plant. The endosperm is a supply of stored carbohydrates, oils, and proteins. The seed sprouts when there is warmth, moisture, and air.

When the conditions are right for sprouting, the embryo feeds upon the endosperm until its roots sink into the soil and the little leaves open to the sun.

During sprouting the inactive endosperm is converted into readily available nutrients. If you harvest the crop *after* the endosperm has been turned into vitamins, enzymes, and amino acids, but *before* the embryo consumes the nourishment, you'll have the best food imaginable.

Be careful to select new crop beans and other seeds. Try alfalfa, barley, cranberry beans, buckwheat, fava, kidney, mung, pinto, soybeans, corn, cress, clovers, caraway, celery, dill, fenugreek, flax, garbanzo, kale, lettuce, lentils, mustard, millet, parsley, purslane, pumpkin, peanuts, onions, oats, radishes, beets, safflower, sesame, sunflower, and wheat.

Getting started

Select clean, whole seeds. Seeds earmarked for outside gardens are frequently pre-treated and are unsuitable for growth in water. Seeds suitable for eating can be found in grocery stores, livestock feed stores, or health food stores.

Soybeans, peas, and alfalfa are just about right when their sprouts are 2-3 inches long. Grain shoots such as sunflower, wheat, oats, and rye are best when the length of the original seed. Lentils are best about 1 inch long. Mild flavored mung beans can be grown as long as 3 to 4 inches.

The simplest means of sprouting are as efficient as the costly devices found in the market. Most people use the mason jar method for sprouting. You'll need a lid of stainless screening to put over the jar, just the size to fit into the mason screw ring. You can use nylon mesh but it is less effective.

Sprouted seeds are an inexpensive source of vitamin rich foods, quite tasty, fresh or cooked. The process for sprouting seeds is a simple one: most of the materials needed can be found at home. Each different variety of seed has its own distinctive flavor. Two of our favorites are Garbanzo *and* Radish *which taste much like the mature vegetable.*

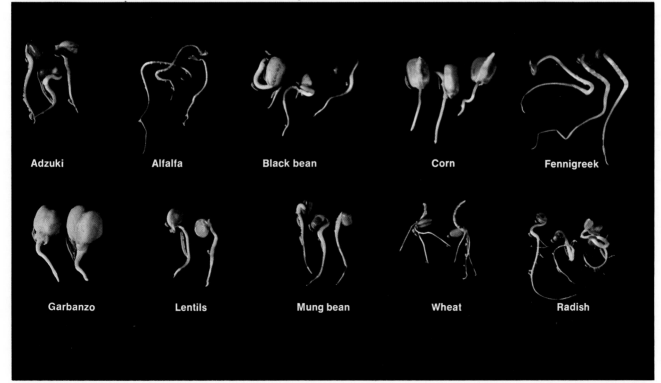

Adzuki **Alfalfa** **Black bean** **Corn** **Fennigreek**

Garbanzo **Lentils** **Mung bean** **Wheat** **Radish**

Homemade sprouters

How to use each is described in the text.

Mason jar — Ring — Wire screen

Earth filled box — Opaque lid — Ground level

Sprouting trays — Opaque lid — Drain holes — Feet — Tray to catch water

Place 2 tablespoons of whatever seed you choose in the mason jar. Fill with water, and soak overnight; any seeds which float on top are probably hollow and should be discarded.

With the jar method use 2 tablespoons of seed to a quart jar. After they soak, drain through the screen lid and put the jar into a dark cupboard. Immerse in water and drain 2-3 times daily until nice sprouts form.

Other methods of sprouting

Wheat or other grain seeds can be sprouted in soil in a little planter. Let the sprouts grow 4-5 inches high and then harvest with scissors; the bottom part is too bitter for most tastes. Sprout cress seeds on a new, damp sponge and harvest with scissors.

One source of information suggests placing pieces of clean brick or rocks on top of the damp padding which covers sprouting seeds. The sprouts will grow extra big, trying to push up under such a heavy weight. I had my doubts, but I found it was quite true, especially with mung beans, which made the sprouts more like the commercial product.

Earth sprouting is another variation. Place the soaked seeds on top of soil inside a wooden box partly buried in the ground. Cover the seeds with fine soil and keep damp.

Some authorities believe the vitamin C yield of sprouts grown in an earth sprouter is nearly double compared to that of seeds sprouted in water.

If the carpenter of the family gives you a hand, try using a stack of small wooden trays for sprouting, made from ¼ -inch wood and treated with wood sealer. (see illustration)

Make a series of about five trays. Punch or drill holes in the bottom of each. Don't forget a top for the stack and feet for the bottom one. Use a pan or tray to hold the stack and to catch surplus water.

Soak, drain, and layer your seeds in one of the trays. Start one tray daily, so you can harvest a continuous crop.

Water 3 times daily, by flushing the top tray, letting the water run through all the trays.

To grow beans in large quantities, put 2 cups washed and soaked mung beans into a tin or wooden pail. Make sure there are holes in the bottom for drainage. Place three layers of coarse cloth (such as sacking) in the bottom and on the top. Place the pail in a dark corner. Sprinkle the beans with warm water 3 times daily. After seven days you'll have an enormous crop. Remember to keep the remaining sprouts damp to keep them fresh and tender.

If you let sprouts sit briefly in the sun, chlorophyll is produced in the leafy portion.

Sprout recipes

Although Chinese cook books have a variety of recipes, don't be afraid to try sprouts in most anything. Use alfalfa sprouts instead of lettuce in sandwiches. Add some to hot soup just before serving. Use in gelatin salads or grind sprouted wheat and include in your favorite bread recipe. Marinate sprouts in French dressing, drain, and use as a salad.

And of course there is always Egg Fu Yung. Coarsely chop a handful of bean sprouts per person. Add chopped green onions, bits of leftover meat, salt and pepper to taste, and 1 to 2 eggs per person. Mix together and make into little pancakes. Cook in a well greased skillet.

For sauce use 1 cup beef stock (or 1 bouillon cube and a cup boiling water), 2 teaspoons soy sauce and 4 teaspoons cornstarch dissolved in a little cold water. Cook together for 2-3 minutes. Garnish the dish with green onion slices or a bit of shrimp or sliced meat, or try this garnish:

Over a medium to hot fire heat 1 tablespoon sesame seeds in your smallest iron skillet. Stir continuously, letting the seeds brown lightly. They almost pop, like popcorn and fill the room with the most delicious aroma. A delicious touch for Egg Fu Yung or any other Chinese dish.

Add sprouts to mixed meat and vegetable dishes a few minutes before the dish is done. For a separate vegetable, sauté a few chopped green onions in a little butter. Add bean sprouts, sprinkle with soy sauce, and sauté about 2 minutes longer.

Fried bean sprouts with pork

½ **pound pork**
2 **tablespoons soy sauce**
1 **teaspoon cornstarch**
4 **tablespoons salad oil**
1 **leek, chopped**
½ **pound bean sprouts**
1 **teaspoon sugar**
2 **additional tablespoons soy sauce**

1. Slice and soak the pork in soy sauce and cornstarch.

2. Heat the oil and fry pork with chopped leek, or some green onions until the meat barely *begins* to change color.

3. Add bean sprouts, sugar, 2 more tablespoons soy sauce, and stir fry, cooking until slightly done, keeping the sprouts crisp.

4. Serve over hot steamed rice. Like most sprout recipes, this is a fast, easy recipe.

Sourdough cookery

Sourdough is very interesting and is an ancient method for rising bread; a sort of wild yeast tamed and put under control. There are a couple of things to keep in mind; first, the sourdough starter has to be fed, or used often enough to keep it happy, and you must always save a little of the starter each time you use it.

Making a starter—if you can't get one from a friend

Mix 4 cups flour, 2 tablespoons sugar, 1 tablespoon vinegar. Add enough water to make a light batter, and cover it lightly with something porous like cheesecloth and let stand in a warm place until it begins to bubble and work, giving off a pleasant odor. The ingredients pick up or attract wild yeasts in the air. Occasionally the original starter will get a bad start and begin to have an awful odor; just throw it out and begin again.

The basic batter or sponge is usually made the night before. Mix 2 cups warm water and 2½ cups flour with 1 cup starter. Let it stand overnight in a warm place. Cover with a clean cloth. In the morning remove a cup of the sponge, before you add anything else to it, to save as your starter. Refrigerate between uses.

Sourdough pancakes

For pancakes, add to the remaining sponge (about 4½ cups), 1 egg, 2 tablespoons oil, ½ cup milk, 1 teaspoon each salt and soda, and 2 tablespoons sugar. I prefer to dissolve the soda in a little bit of water and add it after it has dissolved. Let the batter rest for 5 minutes while the griddle is heating, and grease it well. Drop the batter by the tablespoonful for nice sized pancakes.

Sourdough pancakes require a hotter griddle than ordinary pancakes. Blueberries can be added to the batter for a special treat.

Sourdough biscuits

1 cup sourdough starter
1 cup water
2½ cups flour
2 tablespoons sugar
1 teaspoon salt
1 teaspoon baking powder
1 teaspoon soda

1. The night before, mix the starter, water, and flour.

2. The next morning, recover some of the starter for next time and mix the sugar, salt, baking powder, and soda (dissolved in a little water) into the remaining starter.

The unusual flavor and texture of sourdough bread has made it a popular, if somewhat mysterious, product. The sourdough starter takes advantage of wild yeast from the air. Cast iron french bread pans make the classic shape loaf.

3. Sprinkle a little flour on a board and knead the dough about 20 strokes, pat out to ½ inch thickness and cut into squares or rounds.

If you like soft biscuits, place the rounds of dough on a greased cooky sheet, sides touching. For crisper biscuits place on greased cooky sheet, leaving space in between. Bake in 425 degree oven for approximately 15 minutes.

Another way to replenish the starter

Begin with 2 cups of starter. Mark a 2 cup line on the side of its container with a marking pen or grease pencil.

After you remove any starter, mix equal portions of water and flour together and bring the starter back up to the 2-cup line, stir well, and leave the container out of the refrigerator until it starts working, or bubbling. Refrigerate until you use it again.

Another starter

Put 2 cups flour into a jar or crock, add 2½ cups lukewarm water, and set the whole batch in a warm place, lightly covered.

Still another

Mix 2 cups flour with 1 package dry yeast stirred in and enough lukewarm water to make a thick batter. Let stand in a warm place for 24 hours.

Yet another

Use warm milk instead of water, using the same method as above. Raw milk right from the cow is another milk version.

Positively the last starter

Let a cup of milk stand for a day or so in an uncovered container at room temperature. Then add 1 cup flour, mix and let stand for another couple of days or until it begins working.

It takes several hours for yeast to start growing under ideal conditions, (around 80 degrees). You will have to experiment to find just the right place for making the starter. Remember to take the starter out of the refrigerator so it can warm up a bit before using. And don't forget to save some of the starter, or to replenish it as you use it.

There are several fascinating books available, entirely on the subject of sourdough. Seek them out for some truly remarkable recipes for French bread, cakes, and many other exciting ideas. They are fascinating reading.

Milk products

How to turn milk into something extra; recipes and ideas for yogurt, cottage cheese, cheese, and custards.

Yogurt

An important part of making successful yogurt is an inexpensive styrofoam cooler. They don't hold up very well under hard use, but will last practically forever if you use it just for rising bread or making yogurt.

Heat 1 quart of milk to 170 degrees. (Use a thermometer to be sure.) Pour several inches of 130 degree water into the bottom of the cooler. Let the milk cool to 130 degrees and add ⅓ cup commercial plain yogurt. Mix well and pour into small containers with lids. Place the containers in the cooler. Make sure the cooler lid is tight and leave for 6-8 hours, at which time the yogurt should be thick enough to take out and refrigerate.

If this batch is too thin, next time blend in 1 cup of instant powdered milk before adding the yogurt. The dry milk makes a much thicker, creamier yogurt.

Armenian yogurt

A rich creamy version, not recommended for skim milk drinkers. Bring 1 quart of milk and 1 cup of cream to a boil and simmer gently for 15 minutes. Cool to 120 degrees and blend in ¼ cup yogurt as a starter. Leave in the cooler, as in the original recipe, until very thick. It will thicken in 4-5 hours. Refrigerate after yogurt is the desired thickness.

Fruited yogurt

Before placing in the cooler, add ¼ cup fresh or frozen fruit for each 2 cups of yogurt you are going to make. The fruited yogurt tends to develop more quickly than the plain variety, so check for doneness a little sooner.

Yogurt made in a thermos jug

If you do not have a cooler, try making yogurt in a wide mouth thermos jug. Bring the milk and yogurt culture to 110-130 degrees and pour into the thermos. Seal and leave for 3-4 hours. If it is not thick enough, leave it for a while longer. When done remove the lid and chill in the refrigerator.

Cottage cheese

You can make cottage cheese with pasteurized milk from the store or from raw cow or goat's milk. One gallon of milk makes about 1 quart of cottage cheese.

Place 1 gallon of milk into the top of a double boiler. Using a dairy thermometer, bring the milk to 76 degrees. Add ½ cup buttermilk to the milk. Stir thoroughly and let stand until it thickens like custard and let stand for up to 24 hours. Keep it covered and in a warm place. When it is hard, cut into 1-inch cubes. Let the curds stand without stirring for 15 minutes. Slowly bring the curds and whey to 120 degrees in the double boiler. Keep the curd at the 120 degrees for about 30 minutes, stirring occasionally. Do not overcook or overheat the curd.

Pour the hardened curds into a cheesecloth-lined strainer. Rinse by dipping the strainer into cool water, once or twice. Pull the ends of the cheesecloth together to form a bag, and let the cheese drip for an hour or two. Season with salt and white pepper.

For a similar recipe bring one gallon of milk to 76 degrees. Add ½ cup buttermilk and 1 dessert rennet tablet dissolved in one teaspoon cold water. Stir in well and leave in a warm place at the 76 degrees for 12-18 hours. The use of the rennet makes a larger and sweeter curd. At this point follow instructions from the previous recipe.

Armenian soft cheese

Heat to lukewarm in a double boiler, 3½ quarts milk and 1 pint cream. Add 2 dessert rennet tablets dissolved in cold water. Stir, and let stand until thick. Stir, and let stand for another 10 minutes. Leave and then stir a third time. Drain in a jelly bag or cloth-lined strainer, squeezing out as much whey as possible. Leave the cheese in the bag and cover with a saucer. Weigh it down with a couple of books and leave for 4 hours. Remove from the bag, cut into 4-inch slices, and salt lightly. This is a light breakfast cheese, similar in taste to hardened cottage cheese.

Cup custard, steam method

This recipe shortens the custard cooking time considerably. Makes 5 servings of ½ cup each.

  2 eggs
⅓ **cup sugar**
¼ **teaspoon salt**
  2 cups milk
½ **teaspoon vanilla**
  Freshly grated nutmeg

1. Beat eggs with sugar, salt, milk, and vanilla.

2. Pour into 5 custard cups and sprinkle with nutmeg.

3. Pour about 1 inch of water into a skillet and bring to a boil.

4. Reduce heat to a low simmer and place the cups in the skillet.

5. Cover loosely and cook for 15-25 minutes or until a silver knife inserted into the edge of the custard comes out clean. Chill and serve.

If you have a steamer, try using it and stand the cups of custard on the steamer insert. Cover with the steamer lid and steam as long as you cooked the skillet custard.

A delicious and nutritious dish, especially for children. Unless you let the heat get too high and the custard separates a little, they look and taste just like oven baked custards.

Homemade root beer

The easiest way to make root beer at home is to start with a commercial root beer extract and follow the attached directions. One small bottle of the extract makes nearly five gallons of root beer, so before you consider making any, know how many bottles you have, or can get, and be sure that the number of bottles total 160 ounces. You can use old soda pop bottles or beer bottles, but make sure they all use the same type of cap. (Don't use the screw-type bottles.)

The bottles have to be washed, soaked, and sometimes washed again, to get out any dirt that may have accumulated in them. Rinse well to get rid of any left over soap. I purchased a very bristly, long bottle brush from a wine supply house which is a real time-saver for the hard to clean bottles.

The root beer recipe uses four pounds of sugar as a food for the

A favorite summertime activity—making root beer—is easy once you round up enough empty bottles.

yeast and for sweetening the root beer. The recipe also calls for one half teaspoon of yeast—*do not add more:* Follow the warnings and use only the amount recommended.

In days past, my husband's father used to make gingerale and root beer, and double the yeast, or just not measure it carefully. He has childhood memories of bottles exploding in the basement during a hot spell, and having to clean up glass afterwards. The product was delicious, but a little worrysome; like walking through a mine field.

We only make root beer when we expect nice warm weather for about five days in a row. The root beer turns out better if the weather is consistently warm for several days, as the yeast must keep growing at a steady rate. Friends of ours have tested the temperature of a cupboard over their refrigerator and found it had controlled temperature all the time, and now make their root beer there year 'round.

After four or five days shake a bottle gently; it should have nice fizzy bubbles. Put a few into the refrigerator to chill and taste. If it hasn't gone quite long enough, wait another day or two and chill and taste another bottle. Keep testing until it tastes just right. Try homemade root beer over homemade vanilla ice cream for the best float ever.

Making soap from lard

To make homemade perfumed soap, spread 10 pounds of lard approximately 1 inch thick on a board. Place blossoms deep into the lard. Choose bright smelling blooms for the best effect and keep the board in a well sheltered area outside. Leave the blossoms in the lard for 24 hours, and then remove. For a stronger fragrance, add new blossoms and leave for another 24 hours.

For a pine needle odor, boil pine needles in soft water for 5 minutes and let steep for another 10 minutes. Strain and use this water in place of the plain water needed in the soap recipe.

Put the 10 pounds of lard in a kettle with 2 quarts of soft water (or the pine scented water) and bring to a boil. Cool overnight. Any dirt or meat particles will sink to the bottom and can be scraped off easily the next morning.

Mix 4 tablespoons sugar, 2 tablespoons salt, 6 tablespoons powdered borax, and ½ cup ammonia into 1

Almost a lost art, homemade soap puts rendered lard to good use. 1. A mixture of borax, ammonia, lye, and water is poured into the lard. 2. & 3. After the soap has thickened it is poured into a form, lined with a damp cloth for easy removal. 4. Left to dry and harden (the longer the better) the soap is removed from the form and cut into bars.

cup of the pine or soft water. In an outside area mix 2 quarts of cold (soft or pine-scented) water with 2 cups of lye (be sure to read the lye label and follow all precautions and directions for use). Use a stainless steel or graniteware pan. Mix and let the mixture cool to lukewarm. Take the sugar, salt, borax, ammonia mixture, and pour into the cooled lye and water mix. Add the cool lard, slowly, stirring with a wooden spoon. Stir gently and completely until thick and light in color.

Pour the thickening soap into a stainless steel or granite pan or a wooden box lined with a dampened cloth. Leave until hard and cut into portions. The longer you let it dry, the longer each bar will last.

The easiest soap I know

Mix 5 pounds fat (bacon grease is fine), 1 can lye (13 ounces), 6 quarts cold water, and 3 tablespoons borax in an enamelware pan. Leave for 48

hours, stirring frequently with a wooden spoon.

After the 48 hours heat over a low fire until melted. Pour into a shallow box or a heavy and shallow cardboard box lined with a wet cloth. I let the edges of the cloth hang over the outside so it is easier to pull the soap out later.

When the soap is hard, pull it out and cut it into bars using a knife or a wire used as a saw.

The soap will last much longer if you store the bars for several weeks before using. I find that homemade soap lasts so long I get tired of looking at the same old bar. It is white, has a clean smell, and nice to use. I often store it with sachet so it picks up a nice scent. You can also use homemade soap for the laundry. Shred it and dry the flakes in a dehydrator or in a warm place on a screen. It works best in soft water. I like to wash wool for spinning in this homemade soap.

Camping and special outings

Over the years I have found that one of the best places to find the supplies we need for camping trips, picnics, and spur of the moment outings, is right at home.

A camper preparing dinner from inside his tent; a neat trick used during bad weather.

When neighbors call and invite us to a potluck, I look first to the freezer for a casserole or perhaps a cheesecake or cookies to share. The pantry of canned goods always holds jars of beans or sauerkraut that can be chilled for a barbecue salad. Canned peaches or apricots can be made into a cobbler or deep dish pie without much fuss or advance warning. A jug of apple cider or root beer is a good start for a spontaneous picnic; with the addition of cheese, a loaf of whole wheat bread from the freezer, and some dried fruit and nuts, we're ready to go.

After we began drying food, our menus for both car camping and back packing became more interesting when we realized we could prepare many of the foods needed ourselves. A high mountain trip prompted our first experience at making jerky (see page 58) and an expedition the following summer prompted us to turn jerky into pemmican (see page 58). Dried fruits and fruit leather (page 54) had always been outdoor favorites, but we were even more pleased when we could turn some of our dried vegetables into camp stews and soups with the addition of canned, dried, or freeze-dried meat.

No matter how good the food, the trip can only be successful if it is well planned. Planning food for car camping is not such an exacting job because you have the room to take along a few extras and there is usually the convenience of a nearby store. For wilderness camping, though, you must know in advance what you will need, when you will need it, and how much you'll need.

Menu planning

My job is to plan the meals; I let the others in the group plan the itinerary and equipment needs. I find that I am less likely to forget some key ingredient if I know I am the only one responsible.

I write down a menu for each meal needed on the trip, making note of snacks and drinks as well. Besides each menu I write down the necessary quantities of staples as well as any seasonings or cooking fats that may be needed. This is when I try to plan the menus around what we have on hand, plus any new ideas the family may suggest. The meals are kept simple, but they provide us with the basic daily requirements.

We have sometimes made mistakes on the amounts of food and found that small children, who eat like baby birds at home, eat like vultures in a high mountain camp, sometimes getting into food meant for another meal. Anticipate before leaving and remember to plan generous portions for everybody. When you are camping at a high altitude or in cold weather you need extra calories just to stay warm, and increased appetites are generally the rule.

Packaging wilderness meals

When I have all the food on hand, I break it down into the amounts needed for each particular meal. I pack each course separately in a plastic bag (eliminating any cardboard cartons), and then put all the small plastic bags for that meal into a larger plastic bag. A slip of paper goes inside as well, listing special instructions. For example directions may read: Sunday dinner, Chicken Noodle Soup, Beef Stew (4 cups water, 10 minutes), Fruit Cobbler (soak apples, add water to biscuit mix, cook 15 minutes). These abbreviated instructions are enough to tell me how to cook the meal.

I usually make up these plastic bag food packs for each meal, planning so the heaviest food is used first. Staple items such as sugar, seasonings, margarine or cooking oil, dried milk and chocolate milk powder, instant coffee, tea, and instant fruit drinks go into a staple bag.

A cloth bag made from a leg of a wornout pair of jeans makes a proper sized skinny bag, great for holding utensils and other small camp needs together in one place. For the bottom seam, sew the cut edge together; add a drawstring at the top.

There are also special cartons to hold eggs safely, and toothpaste like tubes with a bottom opening and a wind up key, just right for mustard, mayonnaise and the like. These small conveniences can make a real difference on camping trips especially if you're backpacking.

Our anticipation mounts as the bags of food are piled on the table and each meal is assembled. I keep a master list of what we will be eating and which person is carrying it in their pack. I also make a list of fresh things to put in at the last minute.

Breakfast ideas
Instant oatmeal in a cup

  4 cups quick-cooking rolled oats
  ½ teaspoon cinnamon
  ¼ cup sugar
  ⅔ cup instant low-fat dry milk
  ½ cup chopped dried apples (or any other dried fruit)

At home, toast quick-cooking rolled oats in a 300 degree oven for 20 minutes. When cool add remaining ingredients. At camp pour cereal into cup. Pour boiling water in and stir for 1 minute before eating.

Swiss style cereal

A fine food to take camping or backpacking . . . much like the commercial product with a similar name.

1 cup whole filberts
1 cup whole blanched almonds
3 cups quick-cooking rolled oats
¾ cup sweetened wheat germ
1 cup dried currants
⅔ cup dried apricots, finely chopped
¾ cup brown sugar, firmly packed

1. Toast nuts on a baking sheet in 300 degree oven until lightly browned. Rub filberts to loosen some of the brown skin; chop both nuts coarsely. Combine with remaining ingredients.

2. Blend well and pack in a plastic bag. At camp when ready to serve add dry milk powder to each serving and stir in enough water to desired consistency.

3. For cold mornings, pour hot water over this cereal. Also good with stewed fruit. Makes 8 cups.

Golden crispy cereal

4 cups oats
2 cups wheat germ
1 cup sesame seeds
1 cup chopped walnuts
½ cup coconut
¾ cup brown sugar
¾ cup oil
⅓ cup water
2 tablespoons vanilla

Mix all ingredients together and spread in a shallow pan. Bake in a 350 degree oven 1 hour, stirring often.

Fruit mix cereal

5 cups oatmeal
¼ cup brown sugar firmly packed
½ cup salted soy beans
⅓ cup oil
⅓ cup honey
¼ cup raisins
½ cup chopped dried apricots
½ cup chopped dates
½ cup chopped walnuts

Mix all ingredients together except fruit and nuts. Bake on a baking sheet in a 350 degree oven stirring often until done, about 20 minutes. Cool and add the fruit and nuts.

Pruneola cereal

Another breakfast cereal that eliminates pot washing.

1 pound quick-cooking rolled oats
1 cup shredded coconut
1 cup unblanched almonds, coarsely chopped

1 cup sunflower seeds, hulled
1 cup wheat germ
1 cup sesame seeds
½ cup salad oil
1 cup honey
2 cups prunes, pitted and cut in small pieces

1. Combine first six ingredients. Mix salad oil with honey, heat and pour over oat mixture. Mix well.

2. Spread in a large baking pan. Bake in a 325 degree oven for 25 minutes, stirring often.

3. Remove from oven, add prune bits, and cool. Makes about 14 cups cereal.

Breakfast in a cooky

Bake at home and freeze until you make the final assembly of camp food. If you are car camping, serve with hard boiled eggs, cooked the night before in the water heating for dish washing.

⅓ cup whole bran cereal
½ cup orange juice
1½ cubes (¾ cup) butter, softened
¼ cup sugar
1 egg
¼ cup honey
1½ teaspoons vanilla
1 cup flour
1 teaspoon baking powder
½ teaspoon soda
½ teaspoon salt
⅓ cup non-fat dry milk
2 teaspoons grated orange peel
1 cup rolled oats
1 cup chopped nuts
1 cup raisins

1. Combine cereal and orange juice in a bowl. Let stand.

2. Cream butter, sugar, egg, honey, and vanilla. Blend with the soaked bran cereal.

3. Sift flour, baking powder, soda, salt, and milk into bran mixture. Add grated orange peel, rolled oats, nuts and raisins.

4. Mix well and make drop cookies.

5. Bake in a 375 degree oven for 10 to 12 minutes or until golden brown. Makes 4 dozen easy to pack cookies.

All-purpose camp mix

For leisurely camping when you don't mind washing pots and pans, take along the following "All-Purpose Camp Mix." It can be used to make pancakes, biscuits, or cobbler.

9 cups all-purpose flour
1 tablespoon salt
¼ cup baking powder
2 cups shortening

Sift together flour, salt, and baking powder. Add shortening and cut in with a pastry blender until the mixture resembles coarse meal. Double bag in heavy duty plastic bags.

Pancakes

1½ cups "Camp Mix"
1 tablespoon sugar
¼ cup dry milk
1 egg
1 cup water

Blend dry ingredients together. Add egg and water, mix well. Cook on hot griddle until golden brown. (A small 8-inch wire whip is handy for mixing pancake batter and instant pudding, and many gravies you might make in camp.)

Serve pancakes with fruit syrup or maple syrup (see page 31) or honey butter made at home. Whip together equal parts of honey and butter. Pack in a plastic margarine tub.

Bread on a stick

Children enjoy making this camp treat. It takes a little patience to cook slowly so the outside doesn't burn before the middle cooks. Add enough water to Camp Mix to make a stiff dough. Shape the dough into ribbons as thick as your little finger. Peel the end of green sticks about as thick as the child's thumb. Heat the sticks over a low campfire briefly, flour, and wind the ribbon of dough in a spiral around the end of the stick, pinching the dough together so it won't unwind. Toast over hot coals, turning to bake evenly. Slip off the stick when done and fill the hole with butter and jam.

There are lots of cooking tricks that please children on lazy camp days. Try cooking an egg on a hot greased rock, using a piece of bread with a hole torn out of the middle to keep the egg white from spreading. Or cook an egg in an orange. Cut off the top part of the orange and eat the fruit. Drop a bit of butter in the empty orange shell. Break an egg or two inside the orange cup and set on low coals until the eggs are cooked.

Lunch ideas

For pack trips, lunch is basically the same each day. Salami or jerky, cheese, dried fruit, pumpernickel bread or bagels or non-crumbly crackers such as Triscuits or Rye Krisp, nuts, hard candies, and instant fruit drinks. For long trips I determine how much cheese we will need each day and cut it into blocks before leaving home. I dip each block in paraffin (see page 67) to completely cover and seal out the air. We enjoy a variety of our home dried fruits and find dried persimmons and pineapple a nice change from the apricots, peaches, prunes, pears, and raisins.

When backpacking, light weight foods and planning meals in advance are necessities. The well-packed pack includes plastic bags which contain all the ingredients for an individual meal. Instructions are included in the separate bags.

Bean sprouting

Sprouting beans on a camping trip is an idea worth trying. The fresh crunchy sprouts are a nice balance to a concentrated lunch.

Take along two plastic bags for sprouting. Soak the beans overnight in one bag, then pour into a perforated bag. Drain, wrap, and store deep in your pack away from any light. During the day, soak and rinse them at least once. Rewrap quickly and return the sprouting beans to the dark. It takes about 2-3 days to get a batch of alfalfa sprouts (see page 75) so start one bag each day and you'll have a continuous supply.

Trail snack

A good tasting, quick-energy snack.

2 cups chopped almonds
2 cups chopped walnuts
2 cups chopped dried apricots
1 cup raisins
1 cup pine nuts
1 cup sunflower seeds
½ pound dried carob candy bar, or
**   chocolate chips**

Combine all the ingredients at home and package in small plastic bags.

Camp candy

Make this favorite treat before leaving on a trip; a welcome surprise in camp.

½ cup peanut butter
½ cup honey
½ cup carob powder
½ cup shelled sunflower seeds
½ cup sesame seeds
½ cup soy grits
¼ cup wheat germ

1. Combine all ingredients and mix well. Flatten mixture on a greased platter.

2. Roll into small balls or cut into cubes, then roll in shredded coconut, chopped nuts, seeds or powdered sugar.

3. Package in plastic bags for each day's ration.

Dinner ideas for car camping

If you're camping with a store nearby, or camping in your car, you can take a few liberties in the meal planning and cooking procedures.

Camp cheese fondue

Assemble the dry ingredients at home and package in a plastic bag. When you get ready to serve this in camp, be sure everyone is seated as it doesn't take long to prepare.

2 pounds Swiss cheese
3-4 tablespoons flour
1½ cups dry white wine
2 loaves French bread
**   Skewers or fondue forks**

1. Grate the Swiss cheese and toss with the flour until lightly coated. Put this mixture into a plastic bag until ready to use.

2. Carefully heat the wine in a heavy pot until it bubbles. If you cannot control the heat easily, rig up a double boiler to avoid burning the cheese. Mix in the cheese, stirring constantly, until melted. Add a little more wine if the cheese thickens too much.

3. Cut the French bread into chunks. Each person spears a piece of the bread and dips and swirls it in the cheese. Serve fresh fruit for dessert.

Snow Ice Cream

It is well worth making a trip to the snow each year just to try your luck at making snow ice cream. Empty a can of evaporated milk into a bowl. Add two tablespoons sugar for a small can and four tablespoons to a big can. Add a dash or two of salt and a generous amount of vanilla, powdered sweet cocoa or instant coffee. Quickly stir in fresh snow to taste. More sugar and flavoring can be added until you get it just right. More snow can be added, as well, until the ice cream reaches the desired thickness. The best snow for ice cream is the type with light dry flakes, not the granular type.

Camp chowder

A good pick-me-up when the wind begins to blow and temperature drops.

4 slices bacon
2 chopped onions
4 cooked potatoes, cubed
1 can minced clams
2 cups water
2 cups milk
  Salt and pepper

Cook the bacon in a heavy pot and remove. Brown the chopped onions in the fat. Break bacon into bits and return to the pot along with the cubed potatoes, the minced clams and water. Add salt and pepper to taste. When nice and hot add milk. Heat, but do not let boil.

Camp potato salad

  4 potatoes, boiled and cubed
½ onion, chopped
Equal amounts:
    hot bacon grease and vinegar
    Salt and pepper

Mix the cubed potatoes and onions together. Toss with equal amounts of bacon grease and vinegar. Add crumbled bacon, if you have it. Season with salt and pepper. Serve warm.

Campfire Cabbage

Cabbage travels well on camping trips; we have kept it for well over a week without any spoilage. Wash and shred a small head of cabbage. Dice one small green pepper. Cut three strips of bacon into small pieces and brown in a pan over the campfire. Add the cabbage and green pepper stirring to coat the vegetables well with the bacon fat. Cover the pan tightly and simmer just five minutes, until barely tender. Do not overcook. Serve while still a bit crunchy for the most vitamins. Season to taste with salt and pepper.

Aluminum foil packages

These little bundles work like a miniature pressure cooker, steaming the food and blending the flavors. No pans to wash and the packets can be put right on top of the plates for careful opening and eating. Use heavy duty or double wrapped foil.

Hamburger and vegetable packets

4-6 hamburger patties
  1 onion, sliced
  1 potato, thinly sliced
  1 carrot, sliced
  1 celery stalk, sliced
Sauce ingredients:
  ¼ cup vinegar
  ¼ cup catsup
  ¼ teaspoon Tabasco
  1 tablespoon Worcestershire sauce
  ½ teaspoon mustard
1½ teaspoons lemon juice
    Salt to taste

1. Place hamburger patties on separate pieces of heavy foil. Add a few onion, potato, carrot, and celery slices on each patty.

2. Form a cup with the foil. Mix the sauce ingredients together and spoon about 2 tablespoons over each package, seal up the edges tightly, and place on grill and cook for about 30 minutes.

3. Serve immediately. The metal foil displaces the heat rapidly and you can handle the packages a minute or so off the fire.

Hamburger packets

4 thick hamburger patties
1 package dried onion soup mix
1 potato, thinly sliced, per person
4 tablespoons water

1. Place the hamburger patties on individual pieces of foil. Sprinkle each with ¼ package dried onion soup.

2. Add equal amounts of potato slices to each packet. Cup the foil and add 1 tablespoon water to each.

3. Seal tightly and heat directly on the coals for about 25 minutes.

Tuna packages

1 can tuna
1 teaspoon onion flakes
  Chopped celery
  Mayonnaise
  Hotdog buns

1. Make tuna mixture to taste, using tuna, onion flakes, celery and mayonnaise. Spread the mixture on hotdog buns.

2. Wrap in heavy duty foil and place on a grill over coals and heat 10 minutes.

3. Turn packages over a few times to insure equal heating. For a change add cheese slices.

Sausage potatoes

An interesting one dish meal can be made with baking potatoes, cut in half lengthwise and link sausages. Put a couple of the sausages in between the potato halves, salt and pepper to taste, and wrap them together in heavy duty foil. Place the foil packages directly on coals for nearly an hour to make sure the potatoes and the sausages cook completely. Check after an hour, if the sausage is still pinkish, rewrap, and place back on the coals for a few minutes more.

The sausage adds a sort of gravy; no butter or additional dressing is needed. Can be eaten directly off the foil. The camp dishwasher appreciates the use of foil more than any camper can know.

One pot dinners simplify camp cooking considerably. If served with fruit, a good bread and a salad you can have a nutritious, relaxing meal. Some camp foods can be improved with a little window dressing; try dressing up these one pot meals with a garnish of parsley, tomato wedges, or hard boiled eggs.

One pot dinners

Chicken and mashed potatoes

1 package dried onion soup mix
4 cups water
2 hard-boiled eggs, chopped
1 5-ounce can boned chicken
  Instant mashed potatoes

1. Combine onion soup mix with water and cook until onion flakes are tender.

2. Add eggs, chicken, and enough instant mashed potato to thicken.

3. Add a little salt and pepper. Top each serving with a bit of butter or margarine.

Potatoes and chipped beef

Mix enough powdered milk in water to make 3 cups. Add 1 tablespoon margarine, heat to boiling, gradually stirring in instant mashed potatoes until the right thickness. Add 1 package chipped beef and taste for seasonings. Use 1 sliced hard boiled egg or parsley flakes for garnish. Serve with hot toast grilled over the fire with butter and jam.

Porcupines

This is a long-standing favorite with children.

1 pound ground beef
1 cup uncooked rice
1 small onion, finely chopped
1 egg, lightly beaten
1 teaspoon salt
¼ teaspoon pepper
2 cans tomato soup
2 cans water

1. Combine first six ingredients. Shape into 16 porcupines (shaped like a football) and put into a pan.

2. Blend tomato soup and water, add to pan of porcupines, cover, and simmer gently for 45 minutes.

Baked apples

Place apples on foil; sprinkle with sugar to taste. Nuts and fruit pieces can be added if you have them. Add a pat of butter to top and wrap the foil around the apple. Bake the packages directly on the coals, about 20 to 30 minutes. Keep them right side up so the filling stays inside. Serve hot.

Surprise whipped cream. Chill a small can of evaporated milk in the coldest place you can find; a running stream or a snow bank works well. Whip the milk to a froth, add 1 tablespoon lemon juice and keep on whipping until it is very stiff. Add sugar to taste and surprise everyone with a fancy topping for a cobbler or baked apples.

Trout

Wrap a trout in strips of bacon and fasten with a small stick. Grill over hot coals until the trout is golden and the bacon crisp. Serve with a little lemon juice, carried in a small plastic lemon.

Sun tea

If you have access to ice, try making sun tea to use for iced tea. Let tea steep (see page 58 for variety of tea) in a glass jar filled with water in the sun. In a hot place, the tea will steep in 15 minutes.

Reflector ovens

You can bake pies, bread, cakes, cookies, potatoes, in fact anything you cook at home can be duplicated in a reflector oven, with a little practice.

The big secret with a reflector oven is to keep it as clean and shiny as possible since this maximizes the reflection of heat.

The best cakes for baking in camp are applesauce, gingerbread, and other moist cakes that don't need frosting. Fruit cobblers are easy to make too. Cook dried fruit with water until tender. Sweeten to taste with sugar and thicken the syrup with a little cornstarch mixed with

cold water. Mix 1 cup All-Purpose Camp Mix with 2 tablespoons sugar and 2 tablespoons margarine. Add enough water to make a biscuit dough. Drop spoonfuls of dough on boiling hot fruit mixture and bake in reflector oven.

Dinner ideas for back packing

There is a wide variety of freeze-dried foods available for back packing; they are expensive but often worth it. Mail order houses and sporting goods stores are a good source for information about these foods.

I try to combine freeze-dried products with our own food that we dry or things that I can pick up in the supermarket. Reading labels on packages of dehydrated and instant dinners found in the store gives me an idea of things that I can put together myself.

For example to make beef stew, package an assortment of dried vegetables in a plastic bag such as carrots, green beans, corn, and potatoes. Prepare a roux for gravy and package with seasonings in a second bag or use a package of gravy mix. Take along freeze-dried ground beef. The vegetables need soaking so put them in a heavy plastic bag and cover with water in the morning. Tie the bag to your pack. The vegetables will be ready to cook by evening. Cook the vegetables and the meat, then add seasonings and roux, and stir until thickened.

Foreign food markets often have interesting things you might never have thought of such as Japanese or Mexican dried shrimp, or Italian dried codfish. Soak them in water during the day and they'll be ready to make into a one-pot meal with the addition of instant rice and packaged cream sauce.

Japanese ramen (pre-cooked instant noodles), though rather bulky, make a nice change. Cook a variety of pre-soaked dried vegetables in the seasoned stock before you add the noodles and add slivers of jerky.

High Altitude Cooking

Cooking time doubles for each 5000 foot increase in elevation, and it takes an age to get something cooked. The only solution I have found is to take a pressure cooker along when cooking at high altitudes. Foods cooked in the pressure cooker take the same amount of time as it would take to cook at home. No regard has to be taken as to the outside atmosphere, all that counts is the pressure inside this handy cooker. At high elevation it

will take long enough just for water to boil without having to wait an age for the meal itself.

When baking any product containing yeast or baking powder it will turn out feathery light at high altitudes. I don't bother adding less of either, I'm just pleased with such light textured bread and baked goods.

Beans and other products that require a long cooking time can be prepared more easily in camp if you soak and precook them for a portion of the cooking time at home and then let dry completely before packaging. In camp soak the beans in water for a short time to reconstitute. The cooking time will be considerably shortened.

The altitude change and a longer time required for cooking makes it necessary to take advantage of some of the precooked packaged meals with instant rice and pastas. Baking takes the same time, it is just the boiling that takes so much longer. So, in higher altitudes, plan more baked meat dishes, or the casserole types, or use a pressure cooker which is one item which is well worth its hauling weight. I take mine on every camping trip, a special one with short stubby handles on both sides.

Safeguarding foods during camping trips

At high altitudes the sun is surprisingly hot and the shade surprisingly cold, so plan accordingly. It's best not to keep leftovers, and run the chance of food poisoning, *unless* you can find a consistently cold place to store them. You might try storing some of the perishables in plastic bags placed in a stream or a snow bank.

Insects are sometimes a problem when camping at lower elevations. Wasps and yellow jackets are particularly worrisome when you are eating. Try putting a little bit of whatever you're eating a ways away from the eating area in hopes of enticing the pests there instead of on your dinner.

In areas where wild animals frequent, special precautions must be taken to protect food from these marauders. Place your food in a bag, tie with a long rope and hang over a tree branch. Tie the other end of the rope to the trunk or a low limb so you can lower and raise the bag easily. Guard against the smaller creatures like raccoons and porcupines by covering any food left in the open with a blanket, weighted down with good-sized rocks. They are most clever in opening those plastic lids on coffee cans and will help themselves to the dessert in no time.

Decorative drying

Some of the old-time methods for creating gifts and decorations using the harvest from the garden

Not everything you preserve from the harvest has to wind up on the kitchen table; many dried products can be made into unusual and attractive decorations. We live in an old house that needs a bit of "prettying-up"; hanging strings of garlic, onions, peppers, and shallots, dried beans or herbs in antique canning jars, dried flower arrangements and "memory boxes," have all made a pleasant addition to our surroundings.

Shallot strings

Sort through the shallots, with stems intact, pulling off the worst looking leaves. I like to peel back the first layer of skin, exposing a "clean" surface. Braid the strands, beginning with three, as you would a young child's hair. Add more shallots in turn, arranging them in an attractive manner.

I tie the beginning and end of the shallot strings with twine or yarn and leave a hanging tassle on each. Hang the strings on a porch, or other breezy, shaded place, for further drying.

If you wait until the shallots are perfectly dry, it is difficult to braid the long stiff stems. Work with them when they're about half-dry and then let them dry completely before packaging or bringing into the house. To use, just cut off or pull the shallots out in turn.

Garlic strings are prepared the same way as the shallots. The long strings of garlic keep a long time, much longer than cloves in a basket or box, as they are completely exposed to the air and continue to dry while hanging.

Onion strings

Use the shallot method for braiding, but sort more carefully because the onions are larger and often have hidden pockets of rot you might overlook. Another way to string onions, is to gather a bunch of them and tie the tops with braided yarn of bright colors.

Pomander balls

Pomander balls can be made by simply pushing whole cloves closely placed, into oranges, lemons, or apples to preserve and sweeten their smell.

For fancier pomanders use a couple of rows of cloves, a row of dried flowers, and several more rows of cloves, making a decorative pattern until the fruit is completely covered. Sprinkle crushed orris root or powdered cloves on the clove heads, avoiding the little flowers if you can. Push in a long wire to use as a hanger.

Pomanders containing flowers will shatter if used in a drawer, so it is best to hang them in a closet.

Dry 3 to 4 weeks before giving as gifts, and check from time to time and replace the cloves if necessary. Children love making pomander balls, but be sure to remind them to place the cloves close together, as the cloves keep the fruit from decaying. If you have any trouble pushing the cloves in the fruit, use an ice pick to make a small start through the rind.

Chili pepper strings

You have to be a little more ingenious to tie the pepper strings. They have short stems and nothing to braid. Knowing a little about macramé knots helps; I use a double strand of heavy twine and tie a square knot around the stem of the first pepper. Start with the string doubled at the top and work downward.

Pepper string

Tie a square knot around each stem

Memory boxes

Memory boxes are particularly good for showing off small "treasures" too little or unimportant to display by themselves. When placed in combination with other items, each in their individual sections, the memory box becomes a real attention-getter.

We have built our own with pieces of scrap wood, or wood from old fruit boxes. If you have any pieces of glass at home, make the box to fit the size of the glass. The boxes can be made with the glass fronts permanently in place, or built so that the glass slides out for a change of scenes.

I have one with a tiny wooden nativity scene, colorful Christmas candies, an antique marble collection, and a little tiny basket full of red winged blackbird eggs abandoned by the mother when the hay was cut. Another has an interesting collection of the different varieties of dried beans we grew last season; an attrac-

Apple dolls, memory boxes, cornhusk dolls, and strings of peppers or garlic make unusual gifts and can be made from materials found around the house or from the garden.

tive contrast of bright purple spotted-white beans, dull ivory soy beans, and mahogany colored kidney beans.

Dried bouquets

No matter how crowded the vegetable garden becomes, there's space for a few strawflowers and other flowers which are well-suited for drying (sometimes called "everlastings").

The following list contains some of the flowers which are best for drying:

Helichrysum Monstosum; a big and brightly colored daisy-like flower.

Globe Amaranth; a ball shaped brilliantly colored bloom.

Acroclinum; a giant flower in shades of red. They must be picked in bud to keep the bright color.

Chinese Lantern Plant; small balloon-like husks which turn to orange-red when dry.

Ammobium Alatum Grandiflora; the branches are wing-like and have white flowers with yellow centers.

Money Plant; silvery-white paper thin pods which look something like silver coins.

Job's Tears; the hard grey seeds are made into good luck necklaces.

Love in a Mist; each flower is enclosed in a lacy foliage.

Statice Sinuata; mixed colored flower clusters.

Xeranthemum; papery double flowers with a range of colors.

Rhodanthe; silvery petals and showy flowers.

Teasel; spine-like brown seed heads.

There are many more, but this is a good collection to begin decorative flower drying.

Pick the most perfect flowers and tie them securely into bundles. Hang them "stem-up" in an airy, dark place for full drying.

A big cardboard box with tissue paper between the flower layers makes for good storage.

Silica gel is a commercial drying agent, excellent in quality, but expensive. It dries flowers in a few days and does not distort the flowers as do some of the other drying agents. The silica gel, which is originally blue, will turn pink with the absorption of moisture from the flowers. You can re-use the gel if you heat it in a 200 degree oven until the crystals turn blue again. Try your garden shop for silica gel, sold under a variety of trade names.

Indian corn

We grow a patch of Indian corn each year, being careful to keep it well away from the regular corn, so there will be little or no pollen transfer.

I generally save some of the more attractive Indian corn for decoration and shell the rest off the cob for table use. I save the husks for tamales and for making corn husk dolls.

If the corn is left in the garden to dry, an early autumn rain can slow up the process and sometimes mildew the husks. If you don't want to chance it, dry the corn in a protected, airy spot.

Gourds

Gourds come in an intriguing variety of colors and styles and are a fascinating project for children to grow. You can buy assortments of seeds in a single package; these packages sometimes produce some real surprises. The luffa or dishrag gourd has a tightly woven inner structure which can be used for a dishrag or bathing sponge, just the right size for scrubbing. Seed packages have instructions for making the gourds into sponges.

Pick gourds when the stems turn brownish. They must be picked before the first frost arrives, even if the stems have not turned. Punch the end close to the stem with a long needle or sharp stick to let air inside for faster drying. Hang in onion sacks for several months in a well ventilated place. The seeds will rattle when the insides are dry.

If some moisture appears on the skin just wipe it away; this is a normal part of the inside drying process. When the gourds are dry, spray or paint with shellac or acrylic spray.

To make bowls and jugs, cut into the dried gourds with a sharp saw and scrape out the insides. Clean out the inside with a pot scrubber and treat with several coats of shellac for a smooth finish.

For bird houses, soften the dried gourd in water and then start a hole with an apple corer, or wood working bit. Sand smooth and hang in the nearest tree.

Amy's apple dolls

Begin with very large, ripe, firm apples. In our area Golden Delicious is a good variety to use. Peel the apple under cold, running water, leaving the stem and some skin around both the stem and blossom ends.

Step 1

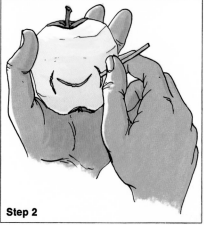

Step 2

Using a toothpick, make slits in the apple that will form the mouth and cheeks. Push the toothpick in fairly deep—especially as you near the center of the mouth.

Soak the apple for about an hour in pure lemon juice. Then tie a piece of string to the stem and hang the apple in a window for the slow drying process which sometimes takes as long as four weeks. Don't put it in direct sunlight—try a north window.

After two or three days of drying, the apple will have softened enough to feel rubbery. Use your fingers and a blunt instrument to start shaping the features. Shape them gradually, a little each day. Press in above the

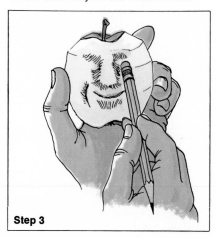

Step 3

mouth cut to form the base of the nose. The cheeks can be pinched into shape on either side. After a few more days form the eye sockets with the blunt tool, pushing toward the center to form the nose.

The forming of the features is a gradual process. Work on it a little each day as it continues to dry. You can build more character into the face if you work slowly. It may pay you to try several apples at one time so you have a better chance of getting a doll face that you like.

When the apple doll head has dried to its final form, in about four weeks, it's time to add the finishing touches. Small black beads for the eyes, small white beads or grains of rice for the teeth, and lamb's wool for the hair. Then a little rouge on the cheeks; some lipstick, applied with a bit of cotton on a toothpick; eyebrows added with eyebrow pencil or felt-tip pen, and your doll is ready for its body.

The body can be made with a corn husk frame. Begin with a wooden chopstick and wrap it with wet corn husks for the trunk. Make arms with corn husks rolled over wire and attach them to the chopstick with a wrapping of corn husks.

When the arms are in place, add more corn husk wrapping for bulk

Step 5

If you want a man doll separate the skirt in half and tie the "ankles" with string, without the full skirt for support, the man doll will not stand by itself, however.

For an old lady, try a full skirt of calico or gingham glued on with a nice tight belt. Put a little ruffle around the neck and cover the entire shoulder and waist area with a fringed piece of cloth—a granny shawl.

Attach the head and work it around until it looks right with the body and the clothes. If the doll you made seems to need hands, you can make them with a wedge of apple cut as shown in the drawing. Soak these in lemon juice, too.

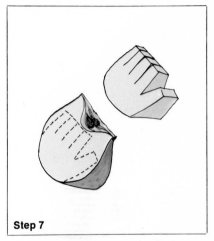

Step 7

Hang them up to dry—they'll dry much faster than the head—and then shape them with scissors and attach them to the ends of the arms.

Glasses for granny can be fashioned from wire and secured tightly where the ears ought to be.

Rose beads

In early colonial days rose petals were made into beads for necklaces. Finished beads are dark brown in color, regardless of what color the original petals were. If you prefer black beads, add rusty nails to the petals as you cook them, or cook in a cast iron pot.

Gather 5 cups highly scented rose petals and barely cover with water. Simmer gently for 2 hours. Stir to break up the petals. Remove the nails if you included them. Leave the petals overnight.

For the next 2 or 3 days simmer the petals to evaporate more and more of the water. Knead well and form individual round or oblong beads, making them bigger than needed because they will shrink some when dry.

Pierce each bead with a thick needle. Center the hole as perfectly as possible. Thread all the beads on wire and hang where they will hold their shape. Move them back and forth daily to keep the stringing hole open. In a week they will be as hard as rock and you can string them onto thread or carve designs in them. The beads retain their rose scent for a long time.

Step 4

and some across the arms to form the shoulders and torso. Make a skirt with bundles of husks—be sure you have enough to support the doll after the head and clothing are added.

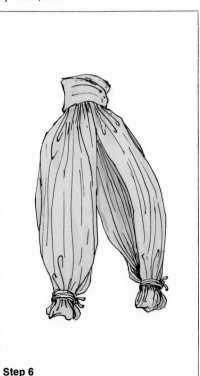

Step 6

And now the clothes. Is it a gentleman farmer, an old lady beggar, or an old witch with a pointed hat? Use small prints or well-worn denim for doll clothes.

Not necessarily necessities

There are some cooks who believe that "they don't make them like they used to," and though the equipment and ideas discussed in this chapter are not necessities—they sure help

◁

Many of the helpful kitchen "aids" from days past can still be found if you know where to look and what to look for. They serve double duty as interesting decorative items and as helpful tools in the kitchen.

An interesting and useful hobby for good cooks today is collecting and using old utensils, useful antiques, and "usable collectibles." I have a special collection of equipment just for my cheese making and sauer-kraut making. I have found that some of the old equipment works better than their more modern counterparts, and in addition has great beauty for display. As an example, an old fashioned kraut-cutter speeds up cabbage cutting and yields thin uniform slices necessary for the best sauerkraut curing. The old-style skimmers, strainers, molds and long wooden spoons are all useful when working with milk products.

Finding some of these older items will take some determination, but by scouting around antique stores, and garage and barn sales, many of them will turn up—*if* you know what to look for. Occasionally you'll find a surprise; at one barn sale we found an old, homemade portable stand for holding gunny sacks open; it made that year's walnut harvest a lot easier.

You might keep your eyes open for some of the following equipment that I have found particularly helpful:

✓Old-style salt holders; if kept next to the stove, they're easier to dip out of and handier than the conventional shaker.

✓Old molds are great for molding jellies, puddings; quite widely available.

✓Antique canning jars with zinc lids, for storing beans and other dried edibles. Too precious to use for canning, but just right for storage purposes.

✓The old tin cookie and cracker boxes make excellent bread boxes—big enough to hold the cutting boards as well.

✓Some of the smaller helpers include peelers, scorers, ornamental cutters of all types, tea balls, corers, scoopers and even cookie cutters can be found at antique and garage sales.

✓The favored, old fashioned, four screen flour sifters may be a little hard to find as they are in demand by today's home bread bakers.

✓Both modern and antique cast iron pots and pans are indispensable. I especially like French bread, gem and muffin pans made of cast iron. I have a large collection of cast iron cooking ware and love the way they cook and bake, preferring them to most any other utensils available.

✓Old fashioned cast iron popover pans make the popovers pop about twice as high as a thin aluminum pan.

✓I use an old fashioned wringer washer to get the soap and rinse waters out of the wool from our sheep. I wash the wool prior to carding and spinning and have found nothing else that works as well.

✓The old rolling pins that hold ice water still work better than any modern type; great for flaky, thin crusts.

✓The old fashioned waffle irons that bake right on the top of the stove are interesting to use and work well.

✓Last of all, how about having a coal oil lamp or two for use during electrical failures?

Coolers

A cooler is a convenient storage area for a few leftovers, jams, jellies, fruit, onions, or potatoes—the kind of food that requires storage temperatures between room temperature and refrigeration. They were very popular years ago; it is interesting to see that they are once again being included in well equipped kitchens in some areas.

They are nothing more than a cupboard with screened or slatted shelves, and screened vents on top

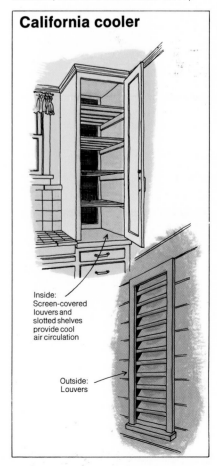

California cooler

Inside:
Screen-covered louvers and slotted shelves provide cool air circulation

Outside:
Louvers

and bottom, letting in cool air from the basement or under the house. The cool air flows through the cooler and out the vents in the ceiling, or attic. Basement air is nice and cool, even in the summer, providing just the right atmosphere for many foods.

The ideal harvest kitchen

I have done a lot of thinking about what an ideal kitchen should be, what it should have in it, and what it would look like. If I could start from scratch, the following ideas would be incorporated into the plan. You may not agree with all the suggestions, but some of the ideas may prove helpful if you ever have the chance to remodel or build your own kitchen.

✓I would like a couple of low, old fashioned tables, just the right height for kneading breads, rolling out pie crusts and cookies. These could be on roll-around wheels and have a couple of tin lined bins for flour and sugar.

✓A separate, small hot water heater just for the kitchen; the fast recovery would be ideal for kitchen work.

✓A dishwasher with an inside arrangement so you could wash jars and lids for canning conveniently.

✓The proper storage facilities for appliances, placed where they are used most often.

✓Over the stove, a big clock with a sweep second hand for those delicate timings.

✓Knives close at hand, as well as other small utensils which are used often.

✓Two sinks would be great; one for regular washing up and one for watering house plants and cleaning vegetables, if you didn't have such an arrangement outdoors near the garden.

✓Bookcases are necessary for the well equipped kitchen, with lots of good cookbooks, and a filing section for all those cut out recipes that we keep thinking we'll have time to try.

✓A desk with a telephone and other business equipment close at hand. Next to the phone, a bulletin board for messages for all the members of the family.

✓Rather than brilliant overhead lighting I would rather have spot lighting in different areas where needed; this would also save electricity.

✓A pantry area, well stocked with your home canned things, plus the herbs and spices stored well away from the kitchen's heat.

✓A big freezer, with all the necessary equipment for wrapping, labeling and

Although the "ideal" kitchen is a matter of personal needs and wants, it is generally a blend of convenience, the proper equipment, and pleasing design. Here a winter squash is being made into squash pie in such a kitchen.

inventory right at the site.

✓Wine racks, in a cool spot, would be nice for those interested.

✓Our family has always enjoyed having the menu for dinner printed on an old blackboard. This could be used as a wall hanging near the dining area.

✓If the kitchen is to be absolutely perfect, you must not forget a warming place for rising bread and making cultured milk products. This could be a cupboard with a light bulb arrangement inside to provide just the right temperature for these jobs.

✓Another idea for bringing beauty into the kitchen area would be a display corner or alcove with ever changing things of beauty. A vase of spring buds, pretty rocks, or just whatever catches your fancy from week to week.

✓But, back to the necessities, how about a non-tarnish lined section of drawers for silverware? I would also need spice racks, easy to reach and easy to identify for fast use.

✓I would use wrought iron pot hangers near the stoves, so that pots and other utensils would be easy to get at, rather than stuck away in a cupboard.

✓I would like some cupboards, open without doors, so that others could view the more attractive dishes and plates and other interesting items. I would also like to have some closed cabinets to hide the clutter and muss, which I have rather a lot of.

✓The counters would have to be made of maple, the chopping block type, with at least a small section of marble for rolling out pie crusts and pouring out candy.

Acid Foods. Foods which contain from 0.36 to 2.35 or more percent natural acid. The term also applies to foods which have been preserved in vinegar. Some examples of acid foods are tomatoes (the *only* acid vegetable, but there are some new "low acid" varieties on the market so be sure to know the variety you are using), fruits in general, rhubarb, pickles, and relishes.

Actual. That part of the formula for any product, containing several ingredients, which refers to a specific ingredient. For example, a 5-pound box of a general-purpose plant food 10-10-10 would have 10% nitrogen, 10% phosphate, and 10% potash. 10% of 5 lbs. is ½ pound. Therefore, the *actual* content of the three major ingredients in the mixture is ½ pound each.

Blanch (steam or water blanch). The process of heating vegetables to the point where the enzymes which cause deterioration are inactivated. To steam blanch a wire basket or colander is placed in a kettle over a small amount (approximately two inches) of boiling water. The vegetables are placed loosely in the colander and a tight-fitting lid is placed on the kettle. Follow directions for individual vegetables for length of blanching time. When water blanching vegetables, the vegetables are placed directly into boiling water; use only enough water to cover vegetables. The blanching time is the amount of time the water is actually boiling. After the vegetables are blanched they are submerged into ice-cold water for approximately the same amount of time they were blanched to stop them from cooking any further.

Bloom (pertaining to fruit). A whitish-colored powdery coating on the surface of fruit, especially prunes.

Bottle Capper. A small hand-operated device for capping bottles with crown caps.

Botulism: A poisoning caused by the toxin produced from the growth of spores of *Clostridium botulinum* in a sealed jar. The spores of Colstridium botulinum are carried from place to place by dust, wind, and the soil clinging to raw foods. These spores can grow in a tightly sealed jar filled with any of the low-acid foods because by nature they cannot grow in the presence of air and they do not normally thrive in acid foods.

The spores are destroyed when low-acid foods are processed in a steam-pressure canner, which is in good working order, for the correct amount of time. Home canners who use the correct methods of selecting, preparing, packing and processing have no reason to worry about botulism.

As an extra precaution, all low acid food should be boiled in an open kettle for 15 minutes before tasting. This step would destroy any toxin which might be present if some error were made in the original processing. Thick masses of vegetables, such as greens, should be stirred and boiling.

Brining. Preserving meats, fish, or vegetables by soaking them in water which has been heavily saturated with salt.

Broadcasting. Scattering a material such as fertilizer or seed evenly over a soil surface.

Catch Crop. A fast growing vegetable crop planted between rows of slow growing crops for best use of space. Also used during the period between harvest of early crops and sowing of late season crops as in *succession* planting or *intercropping*.

Chaff. The husk part of grain and some grasses which is usually separated from the grain by threshing or winnowing.

Check (or "slightly crack"). Prunes picked from the ground are immersed in a hot solution of lye and water. The dip should remove all the bloom, or wax, from the surface of the fruit and slightly *check* or crack the skin.

Cheesecloth. A coarse, light-weight cotton fabric with an open texture, called cheesecloth because it was originally used to wrap cheeses.

Chlorophyll. The green photo-synthetic coloring matter found in plants, particularly in the leaves, where it is continually being manufactured. Known to have a vital role in converting carbon dioxide and water into simple sugars by the process of photosynthesis.

Chutney. A sauce or relish, originally an East Indian dish, made from both sweet and sour ingredients, such as fruits and herbs, with spices or other seasoning.

Cobbler. A deep dish dessert similar to a pie, but without a bottom crust. The top crust is usually made of a biscuit-type dough rather than pastry.

Cold Frame. A box which is not artificially heated but which protects plants from the elements. It is usually covered with plastic or cheesecloth or with a glass sash. Typical dimensions are: 4 ft. wide with a 12-in. front and an 18-in. back. Length is determined by the number of plants to be accommodated. It should be constructed so that it is moveable and can be placed in the sun or shade, depending on the season.

Cold Packing (or "raw packing"). A canning process where containers are filled with raw food or food that has been blanched. The food is then covered with hot liquid, and the containers are sealed and processed immediately.

Compost. A decomposing mixture of vegetable matter—leaves, grass clippings, weeds — which can be used as a fertilizer. Gardeners usually build a compost this way: first a 6- to 12-inch layer of vegetable matter, then an inch of so of soil. Decomposition is speeded up if a commercial fertilizer and lime are used. A practical way is to build up a six-inch layer of material, then cover with an inch of soil mixed with fertilizer and lime.

Controlled Release. A descriptive term applied to fertilizers that release their nutrients in regulated amounts. These are (1) slightly soluble fertilizers that slowly dissolve in the soil, (2) plastic-coated fertilizers through which water slowly penetrates to release the soluble contents, (3) organically incorporated nutrients that are released by microbial breakdown.

Cool Crops. Vegetables which do not thrive in summer heat; e.g., the cabbage family, lettuce, spinach, peas.

Cover Crop. Sometimes referred to as "green manure," a cover crop is useful in large gardens where some of the soil lies dormant in winter. Any of the legumes (clover, cow peas, etc.) sown in fall and turned under in early spring will return valuable humus and nitrogen to soil.

Crock. An earthen pot, jar or other container used especially for brining, curing, fermenting or marinating certain meats, fish or vegetables.

Crop Rotation. Practice employed by both gardeners and farmers for maintaining the good condition of a given section of soil by alternate planting of different crops. Such planting also helps to discourage insects which thrive on a given crop; or diseases indigenous to a certain kind of plant.

Curd. The firmer part of milk, used to make cheese. During the cheese-making process the whey separates from the curd.

Dairy Thermometer. Thermometers constructed especially for the dairy industry which come in various degree levels.

Double Boiler. Actually two saucepans, one set on top of the other. The lower one is filled with water, which, when boiling, heats the upper and cooks food in the top pan without direct heat or fear of scorching.

Drip Irrigation. A system for watering at points on or just below the soil surface so that only small areas are moistened. The irrigation should be made with very low water pressure over a long period of time so as to supply plants with only the amount of moisture needed to replace the plants' moisture loss.

Dry Pack. To package fruits without added liquid or sugar.

Early. A descriptive term applied to certain vegetables that mature faster than others of the same species; i.e., faster growing variety.

Gardening and Cooking
The basic terms

Every activity, be it hobby, craft, or art has its own special language. One of the major problems a novice encounters, in any field, is understanding the language of the more seasoned "pro."

For that reason we have put together some of the basic terms for both gardening and cooking, ones which may have been used in the text without complete explanation or definition.

Keep in mind, though, that reading a definition of a term is no substitute for the experience itself, but it *can* remove some of the stumbling blocks and get you started in the right direction.

Extension Service. A function of the Federal, State and County Cooperative Extension system that provides agricultural and home economics information to residents of the states. Each state has a Land Grant University conducting research and providing educational publications. Most counties have an extension agent, and many have gardening information for distribution.

Follower. A wooden disk used in a cheese press to extract the liquid from the cheese in cheese making.

Fondue. A favorite Swiss concoction taken from the French word 'fondre' meaning to 'melt.' Traditionally made from cheese and wine heated together.

Food Mill. A kitchen device that forces vegetables and fruits through small holes, 'ricing' or puréeing the food.

Freezer Burn. Dehydration of improperly wrapped food, leading to loss of color, flavor, texture, and nutritive value of frozen foods.

Freezer-Life. The time period for which food can be stored in the freezer without losing its flavor and texture.

Freezer Tape. A pressure-sensitive adhesive tape designed to stick tightly at freezer temperatures (when ordinary tape comes off).

Fruit Butters. Are made from fruit pulp and sugar (with or without spices) cooked to the consistency of a thick paste especially for spreading on toast, etc. Less sugar is used for fruit butters than for jams or marmalades.

Fruit Leather. Usually made from slightly over-ripe fruit which has been cooked without water, mashed, resulting in a thick consistency, and spread in a thin layer over heavy plastic or cooky sheets, and dried in the sun.

Fruit Press. An apparatus used to extract the juice from grapes, apples, and other fruit using pressure.

Gasket. A ring made from rubber or metal used to form a water tight, or air tight seal.

Germination. The sprouting of a seed and the commencement of growth. (Also used to mean the starting of plants from seeds.)

Gluten. The tough substance remaining when the flour of wheat or other grain is washed to remove the starch.

Grain Mill. A 'grinder' for converting grain into flour.

Growing Season. The period of time from the last plant-killing frost in the spring to the first plant-killing frost in the fall.

Hardening. A process of slowing plant growth by withholding water, lowering the temperature, or gradually shifting the plants from a more sheltered environment to a less sheltered environment. The process of hardening plants is used to increase chances for survival at transplanting time.

Hardware Cloth. Wire screening such as used for screen doors and windows, only with larger mesh.

Head Space. Space left between fruit or vegetables (usually about ¾ of an inch) and the top of the canning jar to allow for expansion during processing.

Heaving. Occurs in winter as a result of alternate freezing and thawing. The soil cracks and lifts, often thrusting small plants out of the soil and damaging their roots. (May be at least partially counteracted by deep planting or by the application of a mulch.)

Hominy. Whole or ground hulled corn from which the bran and germ have been removed by processing the whole kernels in a lye or lime bath.

Hotkap. A miniature hothouse which can be made in many ways (i.e. using top portion of plastic bottle or a wax paper cone) and used over seeds to force growth by providing additional heat as well as protection from frost, insects, birds, pets.

Husk. The dry, outside protective covering of certain fruits or seeds.

Hybrid. A plant resulting from crossing two plants of the same type which have different individual characteristics for a trait (e.g., tall or short for the height trait).

Interplanting. For the small garden a practical method for getting maximum production and variety by planting fast-growing varieties between slow-growing kinds. A good example is cauliflower planted between rows of corn about four weeks before the corn crop ripens.

Jam. A product made of whole slightly crushed, or puréed fruit boiled with sugar. Although still firm enough to held its shape, jam is usually softer than jelly.

Jelling Point. A test used when cooking jellies to determine whether or not the jelly is done. The test is as follows: Dip a cool metal spoon into the boiling jelly. Lift the spoon about a foot above the kettle and let the jelly pour back into the kettle. The jelly is ready if it divides into two distinct drops that run together and sheet off the edge of the spoon.

Jelly. Made from the *juice* of fruits or berries without any pieces of fruit. It is clear and of elastic consistency because of the pectin found naturally in the fruit, or pectin which has been added.

Jelly Bag. A large square of clean muslin or several layers of cheesecloth through which fruit may be strained.

Jerky. Beef or other meat which has been cut into strips, marinated and dried in a smoker, drying cabinet, or oven.

Lard. The semisolid oil of hog's fat, after rendering.

Long Season Crop. A crop which requires a maximum of frost-free days to produce a satisfactory crop.

Low Acid Foods. Food which contains a small amount of natural acid. Low-acid foods are always processed in a steam-pressure canner. All vegetables, except for tomatoes, are low-acid foods, as well as meats, poultry, sea foods, and soups.

Marinate. Placing meat, fish, or vegetables in a seasoned vinegar and oil mixture for a period of time to improve the flavor of the product.

Marmalade. There is no clear-cut division between the definition of marmalade and jam. The generally accepted distinction is that jams are made from crushed fruits, while marmalades are made from sliced or stripped fruits or whole small berries. A marmalade is a variation of a preserve, usually made from citrus fruits, oranges being the most common.

Masa. A moist dough made from hominy — used to make Mexican tortillas.

Mince. To cut or chop into very small pieces.

"Mother." Scum formed on top of vinegar during fermentation.

Mulch. Any material applied to the soil surface to conserve soil moisture, maintain a more even soil temperature and/or aid in weed control. The mulch may be of manure, leaf mold, straw, sawdust or even paper.

Open Kettle Canning. Used only with jars that have been sterilized and filled with boiling-hot *acid* foods — usually those having a high content of added sugar and/or vinegar; hot covers are put on immediately so that the steam in the contents condenses as the jar cools, shrinking to form the vacuum that completes the seal between jar and cover.

Paraffin. Wax which is melted and used for sealing jars. Used most often in the making of jams and jellies.

Parboil. To boil for a short time, or to partially cook a food, usually vegetables, before further processing.

Pasteurize. A process where a product is heated to 170 degrees and held at that temperature for ten minutes.

Pectin. A carbohydrate found in pulpy fruits which causes fruit to gelatinize when boiled. Slightly underripe fruit contains more pectin than does completely ripe fruit. Commercial fruit pectins are in two forms — liquid and powdered.

Pemmican. A Cree Indian word which, roughly translated, means 'The best food with the most nourishment.' Made from dried meat, fat, and berries.

Plastic Mulch. One of the newer forms of mulching materials. Many polyethylene materials, sold under various trade names, are available either black or clear, slit or solid and in varying widths. Also see Metalized Mulch.

Pomander Balls. Oranges or lemons covered with whole cloves stuck into the rind of the whole fruit. Usually hung in a closet, etc. for the fragrance.

Pone. (Southern) A baked or fried bread made of corn meal.

Preserves. A thick syrup containing whole fruits or large pieces of fruit.

Processing. To cook canning jars filled with food in a water-bath canner, or a steam-pressure canner for the recommended length of time. This cooking, or processing, destroys bacteria, enzymes, molds and yeasts which can spoil the canned food.

Purée. The pulp of a soft food which has been forced through a sieve. If the food is too hard to force through a sieve, it may be steamed or boiled slightly before making into purée.

Quick-Freeze. Food, such as chopped parsley or onions, loosely spread on a baking sheet and frozen rapidly in a cold freezer (minus 10 degrees). When packaged for storage in the freezer the items remain loose which allows for a precise amount to be poured directly from the freezer bag.

Racking. A process of transferring juice, by means of a siphon, into a new clean container, leaving the sediment at the bottom of the original container.

Raw Milk. Milk which has not been treated by pasteurization or homogenization.

Reconstitute. Replacing the liquid which has been removed from a dehydrated food, usually with boiling water or milk.

Rendering. To extract the oil from fat by heating or melting.

Rennet. A substance used in cheese making that speeds the curdling of milk and prevents the formed curd from breaking up easily.

Roux. A mixture of fat and flour heated together and used to thicken sauces.

Row Spacing. Distance in inches or feet between plant rows.

Saltpeter. A mineral salt consisting of nitric acid and potassium used in curing meat.

Sausage Casing. Prepared intestine into which ground meat is stuffed to form links or sausages.

Sauté. A French term which means to fry quickly in a small amount of butter, oil, or other fat.

Scald. To heat a liquid to a temperature just below the boiling point, usually used in regard to milk.

Score. A culinary term meaning to mark a food—a fish, meat, fowl, or vegetables, etc. with small cuts, notches, lines, or strips, sometimes to prevent the food from curling, folding, or crumpling. Sometimes used to make the food more attractive in appearance.

Scum. A film or layer of extraneous matter that forms on the surface of a liquid. Frequently occurs when fermenting or brining vegetables.

Seed Starters. Known commercially as peat pots, Jiffy 7's, Kys Kubes & Fertl Cubes which are small growing units containing nutrients for seed germination.

These can be transplanted directly into soil.

Shelf-Life. The time period for which preserved food can be kept without spoilage.

Short Season Crop. A crop which grows and produces its harvest within one or two months.

Side Dressing. Fertilizers applied close enough to a plant so that its root zone is provided with plant food. Commercial fertilizers should be scattered in a hollow trench parallel to a row, or in a circle around a hill, and thoroughly watered.

Silica Gel. A commercial chemical drying agent used to extract moisture from leaves and flowers for use in dried arrangements.

Spice Bag. A small square of clean muslin or several layers of cheesecloth with spices tied in it so that the spices can be lifted from the liquid they have been cooking in.

Steam Pressure Canner. A kettle which is covered with a tight-fitting lid which also contains a pressure gauge, a vent, and a safety valve or vent. The lid is fastened down with clamps or a system of interlocking ridges and grooves. The canner has a shallow removable rack or wire basket which serves as a rack, which keeps the jars from touching the bottom. Used for processing *all* low-acid foods, under pressure and high heat.

Sterilize. Destroying microorganisms in or on an object, usually done by bringing the object to a high temperature with steam, dry heat, or boiling liquid.

Succession. This means the normal sequence of crops, from cool-weather kinds (e.g., lettuce, peas) to warm-weather varieties (e.g., corn, beans) to cool fall varieties like cauliflower or cabbage. Succession can mean a wide variety of vegetables for one's dinner menu if the gardener plants small amounts of the same vegetable at frequent intervals.

Sulphur Flowers (or "flower of sulphur"). A brand of sulphur used especially for treating fruits before drying.

Water-Bath Canner. A large, deep kettle fitted with a rack and a lid, deep enough to allow one or two inches of water over the top of the jars during processing. The cover on the canner prevents the steam from escaping into the kitchen. (The water-bath canner is generally used for processing fruits, fruit juices, high-acid vegetables such as tomatoes, and sauerkraut, pickles or relishes.)

Weep. Droplets of liquid which form on meringue when it is improperly stored or kept too long.

Wet Pack. To package fruits in sugar syrup, or with plain sugar (which draws juice to form liquid).

Wheat Germ. The embryo or nucleous of the wheat kernel. Contains a concentrated amount of vitamins.

Whey. The watery portion of milk which separates from the curd during the cheese making process.

Winnow. To separate the lighter particles of chaff, dirt, and other extraneous matter from the grain by throwing it into the air and allowing the wind (or wind created with a fan) to blow away any impurities, leaving just the grain.

Altitude chart

Altitude	Pressure Canner	Process at:
2,000 - 3,000 feet		11½ pounds
3,000 - 4,000 feet		12 pounds
4,000 - 5,000 feet		12½ pounds
5,000 - 6,000 feet		13 pounds
6,000 - 7,000 feet		13½ pounds
7,000 - 8,000 feet		14 pounds
8,000 - 9,000 feet		14½ pounds
9,000 -10,000 feet		15 pounds

Altitude	Boiling Water Bath — Increase processing time if the time called for is:	
	20 minutes or less	More than 20 minutes
1,000 feet	1 minute	2 minutes
2,000 feet	2 minutes	4 minutes
3,000 feet	3 minutes	6 minutes
4,000 feet	4 minutes	8 minutes
5,000 feet	5 minutes	10 minutes
6,000 feet	6 minutes	12 minutes
7,000 feet	7 minutes	14 minutes
8,000 feet	8 minutes	16 minutes
9,000 feet	9 minutes	18 minutes
10,000 feet	10 minutes	20 minutes

Common units of value

Unit	Metric System	Avoirdupois System
1 teaspoon	5.0 milliliters	60 drops
1 tablespoon	15.0 milliliters	3 teaspoons or ½ fluid ounce
1 fluid ounce	30.0 milliliters	2 tablespoons
1 cup	0.24 liter	8 fluid ounces or 16 tablespoons
1 pint	0.47 liter	2 cups
1 quart (liquid)	0.95 liter	2 pints
1 gallon (liquid)	0.004 cubic meter	4 quarts
1 peck	0.009 cubic meter	8 quarts
1 bushel	0.04 cubic meter	4 pecks

Index